THE RETURN TO RELIGION

THE MACMILLAN COMPANY
NEW YORK · BOSTON · CHICAGO · DALLAS
ATLANTA · SAN FRANCISCO

MACMILLAN & CO., Limited
LONDON · BOMBAY · CALCUTTA
MELBOURNE

**THE MACMILLAN COMPANY
OF CANADA, Limited**
TORONTO

THE RETURN TO RELIGION

By
Henry C. Link, Ph.D.

NEW YORK

THE MACMILLAN COMPANY

1936

Published March, 1936.

Reprinted June, 1936.
Reprinted June, 1936.
Reprinted June, 1936.
Reprinted July, 1936.
Reprinted July, 1936.
Reprinted July, 1936.
Reprinted August, 1936.
Reprinted September, 1936 (three times)
Reprinted October, 1936 (twice)
Reprinted November, 1936.

PRINTED IN THE UNITED STATES OF AMERICA
BY THE STRATFORD PRESS, INC., NEW YORK

CONTENTS

I

MY RETURN TO RELIGION

I

MY RETURN TO RELIGION

ALTHOUGH in a sense autobiographical, this book is really a condensation of the biographies of thousands of people who have come under my observation. It is the story of many individuals who, in these chaotic times, are groping for the verities of life, for some sure foundation upon which they might rear the structure of their happiness. My own return to religion is unimportant; but my interpretation of their struggles, despairs, and successes may be of major importance, since it is based on discoveries of scientific psychology, many of which have never before been presented to the public in this form.

My return to religion was not due to the depression, although that trying period served to project certain facts into bolder relief. It was not due to old age and approaching senility which often play strange tricks with the mind; as I write, I have just turned forty-five and might therefore be considered in the prime of life. It was not due to ill-health and physical suffering which so frequently turn the attention hopefully to the comforts of a more perfect life hereafter; I am still robust enough to chin myself ten times in succession, to swim a mile, and to eat what pleases me without fear of consequences. My

3

return to religion was not due to misfortune or to disappointments with the affairs of life; on the whole I have been singularly fortunate in worldly matters including sixteen years of happy marriage, three children who have been a source of more pleasure than pain, rather more than average success in my profession, and an income sufficient to satisfy all ordinary needs.

Indeed, there has been nothing sensational or dramatic in my conversion, if I may call it such. There was no one great experience, no emotional cataclysm, no dazzling revelation, which marked the change of which I write. The change was a gradual one, of which I was for a long time unaware. It was due entirely to the routine experiences encountered in the practice of my profession, psychology.

In the professional capacity of a psychologist, I have examined and advised, or assisted in advising, some four thousand individuals during the past fifteen years. These individuals were of all kinds, young and old, men and women, poor and rich. However, with few exceptions, they were normal people with normal problems such as most of us at some time or other have. They were dissatisfied with their present mode of living, had gotten into a rut, or wanted to change their vocations. Some were unhappy in their married life, or were considering a divorce. Some had difficulty in getting along with other people, were unable to make friends, suffered from an excess of timidity. Many had children whose education or discipline and habits presented difficulties. Some suffered from a conflict between their religious beliefs

4

and practices, or from a conflict between their obligations to parents and to themselves. Some had undesirable habits which they were trying to correct. In short, their difficulties were those of normal people to be dealt with from the standpoint of normal psychology. They were not psychopathic cases such as are properly treated by the psychiatric profession in its practice of abnormal or morbid psychology.

In advising such people as a result of my studies of their problems, I found myself more and more frequently using some Biblical expression, or summing up certain recommendations in terms of an accepted religious doctrine. This growing tendency was forced upon me by the realization that my professional and scientific vocabulary was not always adequate. It was neither sufficiently clear nor sufficiently definite for the needs of many who came to me for advice.

I found it a great help in counselling people to be able to reduce a set of scientific or at least partly scientific facts to a few, simple, practical precepts. The frequency with which these precepts resembled the teachings of religion impressed me increasingly as time went on until, finally, I found that I had adopted a large body of religious beliefs most of which I had discarded twenty years ago.

Although I had not attended church more than twenty times in twenty years, I found myself frequently including in my recommendations to individuals that they take a more active part in church work, or join a Y.M.C.A. or Y.M.H.A. There was, for example, the case

5

of a young woman whose immediate problem had been to make a new start in life, away from home, in a vocation which would enable her to support herself. On the basis of certain interests and aptitudes discovered with the aid of psychological tests she had done this quite successfully. Her greater problem, however, was the fact that she had led a self-centered life, and when, after six months, she returned for further counsel, her question was this:

"I still have difficulty in getting along with other people, with men even more than with women. Do you think that I am obstructed by certain inhibitions which might be removed?" My diagnosis was that it was not the presence of inhibitions but the absence of certain desirable habits and skills which were the root of her difficulty. The skills she lacked could be acquired only through practice, not by self-analysis or introspection. So I recommended a specific list of things she was to do, prominent among which was to join a church and to accept all opportunities to become active in its affairs. She had already admitted her belief in religion and her membership in a church in her home town. "Oh!" she exclaimed, "wouldn't it be terribly sordid to join a church just to help me in developing social ease?"

With such a challenge I soon found myself explaining the psychological significance of the Christian religion as exemplified by the social aggressiveness of its Founder and its emphasis on forgetting oneself in the service of others. In her case, the explanation was particularly apt, for her conception of religion had been one

6

merely of believing certain things rather than one of works or service. She had never learned to forget herself in the heat of activity for or with others. In this incident I found myself, practically a pagan, certainly an agnostic, vigorously and with scientific conviction advocating the religious life.

A great variety of incidents like this, some of which I shall relate here, gradually forced me to realize that the findings of psychology in respect to personality and happiness were largely a rediscovery of old religious truths. Paradoxical as it seems, my return to religion was by the road of a science, just as years before the sciences had led me away from religion.

When I entered college I belonged to the Methodist Church and held the religious beliefs of that church. My life from earliest childhood had been strongly influenced by this religion. I had attended Sunday School regularly from the age of four, Sunday church services from the age of six, often morning and evening, Wednesday night prayer meetings, Christian Endeavor, and periodic revival meetings. At one of these meetings, I had gone to the altar as a convert. I became a Sunday School teacher, and I taught Bible classes in the Y.M.C.A. I had in my youth what might be considered an extremely heavy dose of religion.

The small college I entered was known for the fact that eighty per cent of its graduates entered the ministry. There all religious activities were intensified, and yet, because I possessed a genuine craving for knowledge and truth, I found the intellectual atmosphere stifling. The

7

exposure of an intrigue between the president of the college and the dean of women helped to crystallize the doubts of my impressionable mind, and the following year I entered one of our great Eastern colleges, as a sophomore. Two of my first courses were the history of philosophy and religious education.

The history of philosophy was the story of man's intellectual emancipation from the superstitions and blinding beliefs of religion. It described the birth of science through the martyrdom of men who dared to defy the dogmas of the church. It glorified the life of reason as contrasted with the attitude of the early church fathers exemplified by Tertullian, who said: *Credo ergo absurdum est.* That is to say: I believe in the dogmas of the Church in spite of the fact that they are absurd. It contrasted the asceticism of the early Christians and their denial of the finality of this life, with the paganism of the Greeks and their emphasis on the enjoyment of the present. It showed how the forms of religion, the doctrines, the churches, changed in keeping with the shifts of nations and political power. It described the achievements of physics, chemistry, biology and geology which, one after another, revealed the fallacies of religious beliefs. It was about the most illuminating and stimulating course I have ever taken. It was the perfect answer to certain doubts about religion previously aroused in my mind. It gave me a tremendous respect for the powers of reason and for the revelations of science, and it left religion without a leg to stand on.

During the same year, my course in religious educa-

8

tion consisted of a historical view of the development of the Bible. We learned about the piecemeal manner in which the book had grown. Our textbook gave a mass of data showing how one individual after another had rewritten certain parts and added his own trimmings. The passages of the New Testament were split up into three parallel sections, those that were relatively authentic sayings of Christ, those that were historically spurious, and those that were doubtful. This course was a perfect example of what was then known as *the higher criticism* and it made all my previous conceptions of the Bible seem childish.

There is no need to describe all my courses, but one more deserves mention because it was the most popular as well as the most devastating in the undergraduate curriculum. It was the most popular because the easiest to pass, and the most devastating because it upset the religious beliefs of more students probably, than any other course. Strangely enough, it was a course in anthropology. Its high point was the lecture in which the professor drew a small circle on the blackboard and a large circle around it.

"This small circle," he explained, "includes the realm of scientific facts, the things we really know and can prove, the facts of physics, chemistry, mathematics, etc. Between this larger circle and the smaller circle," he said, "lies the field of partly proven facts, of half-knowledge. For example, we can definitely prove the existence of certain chemical elements, and that belongs to knowledge in the small circle. We also have good reason to

9

believe that there are other elements, even though our knowledge of them is uncertain. Such knowledge belongs in the area between the inner circle and the outer circle. Outside this area of half-knowledge lies the whole realm of superstitions, beliefs, and notions for which we have no proof of any kind. The idea of God and the beliefs of religion fall in this indeterminate area. We cannot prove the existence of God, neither can we prove that he does not exist. In respect to this great field, the truly intellectual man can only say, 'I don't know,' that is, be an agnostic."

In all fairness, I must admit that some of my teachers were deeply religious, and that the Sunday chapel which we were then compelled to attend brought us many inspiring preachers. However, the emphasis was naturally on the life of reason, on the intellectual emancipation of the individual. The students divided themselves roughly into two groups, those who did not take their professors too seriously or were too stupid to understand the full significance of what was being taught, and those who were earnest seekers after truth or possessed good minds. The duller the student, the more likely it was that his religion would remain intact, in a logic-tight compartment which his studies failed to penetrate. The more analytical a student, the more penetrating his search for truth, the higher his I.Q., the more likely he was to be stripped of his religious beliefs. I was a Phi Beta Kappa student, and the higher education left me a complete and powerfully fortified agnostic. For twenty years thereafter

10

I scorned the petty practices of the Church, and was convinced that religion was the refuge of weak minds.

And now, a mathematical and quantitative science, applied to people rather than to things, without any conscious awareness of the process on my part for a long time, has completely revolutionized my ideas and values. This science is not to be confused with the popular psychology, in the name of which so many speculative theories have been advanced, including half truths about self-expression, inhibitions, dreams, the subconscious, the libido, the inferiority complex, progressive education, etc., etc. Scientific psychology, which is just as precise in its methods as were chemistry and physics a hundred years ago, is hardly known to the public at large.

The public has heard of an intelligence test or a measure of the intelligence quotient, the I.Q., but few are aware of the fact that well over 1000 different psychological tests have been developed by psychologists and that many of these tests are in daily use. Few know that the Rockefeller Foundation granted one half-million dollars to a group of psychologists to develop the Co-operative Tests now being used in many schools. Few are aware that a staff of psychologists at the University of Minnesota spent five years, on a grant of about 100,000 dollars from the National Research Council and several foundations, developing three tests of mechanical aptitudes.

The public, which spends millions of dollars on musical education, knows practically nothing of the perfection of the Seashore tests of innate musical talent, after twenty-five years of most exhaustive scientific research

11

by Professor C. E. Seashore and a staff of assisting psychologists. Very few people know of the intensive studies by psychologists such as Woodworth, Thurstone, Allport, Wells, Root, Bernreuter, and a host of others, in the field of personality. Both through tests and the clinical use of these tests with individuals, great strides have been made in the understanding of personality and its development. One test of personality traits alone was given to almost half a million people in 1935 in clinics and schools throughout the country and will probably be still more widely used in 1936.

This is the psychology, the findings of which influenced my conclusions in regard to religion, and not the popular and often lurid concepts which go under that name. To this body of scientific psychology I have made certain contributions which have been generally accepted; but the findings I shall report here would not have been possible except for the scientific experiments of many other psychologists. The fact that the results of these studies confirm certain fundamental religious beliefs will inevitably become more generally recognized as time goes on.

As an illustration of the large-scale application of modern psychology to human problems, I might mention the Adjustment Service of New York City which, during the years 1933 and 1934, gave psychological examinations to 15,321 unemployed men and women. On the basis of these examinations the individuals were advised regarding vocations, further training, and in many cases in respect to personality difficulties which were contribut-

12

ing causes in their unemployment. The cost of this service for the sixteen months of its duration was well over two hundred thousand dollars and was contributed largely by the Carnegie Foundation and the Emergency Unemployment Relief Committee of New York City.

I was one of the special advisors in this project, and was also responsible for the planning and supervision of a statistical study of ten thousand of the examinations made.[1] These ten thousand individuals were given a total of 73,226 psychological tests and a comprehensive personal history of each individual was recorded. Since it was just at this time that I began to be aware of the significance of religion in the lives of people, I was able to compare my experiences in individual cases with the mass results made possible by this enormous project. One of these findings, not published in the report, was that the individuals who believed in religion or attended a church had significantly better personalities than those who did not.

My return to religion is not the fervent or emotional return of the prodigal son. Unfortunately, it is a highly intellectual return. It is not something which all religious people would find wholly acceptable, nor do I consider it perfect myself. My concept of religion includes acts which some religious sects condemn, and excludes elements which some sects consider essential.

However, in so far as I can sum up what I mean by re-

[1] See report, Ten Thousand Clients of the Adjustment Service, written by Garret L. Bergen and published by the American Association for Adult Education, New York.

13

ligion, it includes the belief in God as a Supreme Being; the belief in a divine moral order expressed in the Ten Commandments and in the life of Christ, and the acceptance of the Church as the chief, even though imperfect, vehicle of religious truths that are greater than science, and values that are higher than reason. Even this concept may be considered too narrow by the followers of religions other than the Christian religion. It probably is, and I frankly admit the accident of birth which makes it so. But my concern is not with a comparative study of religions. Rather, it is an account of the rediscovery of the values in that religion which I had discarded as having little value.

In practice, I have often encouraged Roman Catholics to be better Roman Catholics, especially in their use of the confessional, which I have found to be of unique value psychologically. I have encouraged many Hebrews to identify themselves more fully with the institutions expressing their religion. In all cases I have been governed by the background and the needs of the individual, and the necessity of utilizing whatever good materials were available.

My return to religion, as an individual, is not important; but the discoveries of scientific psychology which influenced me are. In spite of the great benefits which the physical sciences have bestowed on mankind—a longer life, a more comfortable life, a life more free from physical pains, and a life filled with an infinite variety of interesting objects and educational experiences, there is no evidence that individuals are happier, that families

14

are more united, that governments or political bodies are wiser, or that nations are less likely to go to war.

Indeed, there is much evidence to the contrary. The net annual increase in mental patients in hospitals in the United States has risen to four and one half per cent and the rate is still rising. In 1933 the total number of patient days in all hospitals in the United States for mental cases was 173,000,000 against 123,000,000 patient days for all other diseases. In New York State it has been authoritatively estimated that hereafter one in every twenty-two persons born in the state will go to an institution for mental illness. Such cases represent the extremes of individual failure, but we see their intermediate symptoms in the feverish pursuit of panaceas for happiness which characterizes the whole fabric of our current national life.

In discussing some of these pursuits in the chapters on The Abundant Life and Social Planning, I am not departing from the role of the psychologist but simply pointing out their psychological meaning in respect to the individual. My rediscovery of religion was inspired by the intimate study of individuals, and their problems reflected the characteristic influences of American life. Whether in quest of a vocation, economic security, social satisfaction, or a happier marriage, their salvation lay in a more effective attack on life and society and yet an attack inspired by a truer and more practical set of ideals.

The religion I speak of, therefore, is not the refuge of

15

the weak but the weapon of those who would be strong. I see religion as an aggressive mode of life, by which the individual becomes the master of his environment, not its complacent victim.

II

I GO TO CHURCH

For whosoever will save his life shall lose it: and whosoever will lose his life for my sake shall find it. MATTH. 16:25; MATTH. 10:39; LUKE 9:24; 18:33; MARK 8:35; JOHN 12:25.

II

MY REASON for attending church again is that I have recommended it to so many others. I go because I would rather lie in bed late on Sunday mornings, the only chance for a good sleep I have during the week. I go because I would rather read the Sunday papers. I go because I know it will please my old father, when he learns of it, and my parents-in-law whom I shall undoubtedly see there. I go because I shall meet and have to shake hands with people, many of whom do not interest me in the least; because, if I don't go, my children consider that they have a good reason for not going to Sunday School; because I might be asked to do something I don't want to do; because I may disagree with what the minister has to say. I go because some of my best friends, who know the details of my life, consider me a hypocrite. I go because I do not believe in all the doctrines of this church, or any other church. I go, in short, because I hate to go and because I know that it will do me good.

In my own life I have come to recognize many of the seeds which have sprouted unhappiness and failure in the lives of my clients. Some of them are no longer merely seeds, but flourishing weeds in my character and it is late, but not too late, to do something about them.

19

Now it would be fatuous to conclude that the mere act of going to church is *the* solution to the problems of life, or even that it is absolutely essential to the happiness and success of every individual. I have selected this detail only as a starting point, and this particular detail for two reasons. The first is that one of the basic tenets of the Christian religion and many others is that expressed in the New Testament sayings: "By works was faith made perfect" and "Faith without works is dead" (James, 2: 22, 20). The activities of a church member are not the whole of good works, but they are at least one form of work and certainly one of the most difficult I and many others know.

Hundreds of people have told me: "Yes, I believe in some kind of a God or Divine Being but not in an orthodox way. I don't belong or go to a church because the formal doctrines and practices of the church and its members are repugnant to me." There was a time when I would nod in sympathy with such a declaration, it fitted so well my own agnosticism and withdrawal from the church. Now I realize that this attitude was often a symptom of similar attitudes in other fields of life. My clients believed in friendship, for example, but not in the social activities and personal sacrifices by which friends are made. They believed in a happy marriage but not in the many acts by which it is achieved. They believed in their abilities and aptitudes but not in the routine drudgery by which superiority in any vocation is attained.

The second reason for choosing this as a starting point is that the whole trend of modern, scientific psychology is toward the emphasis on work, on doing things, as the road to happiness, and away from the emphasis on thinking, self-analysis, or talking oneself out of a difficulty. There was a time, still is to some extent, when practitioners on the fringes of psychology believed that in a year of weekly or daily discussions of the libido, a mother or father complex, suppressed desires and inhibitions, some phobia or fear, the sufferer could talk himself into a cure. No doubt some did. I know a woman who was not sure that she loved her husband, and after three sessions a week for a year with an analyst, finally became convinced that she did.

Almost any method, no matter how absurd or unscientific, will help some people, whether it be psychoanalysis, astrology, numerology, palmistry, character analysis, phrenology, Couéism, New Thoughtism, or any of the thousand and one pseudo-scientific cults which fire the imaginations of people for a time. But at what cost and with what injuries to others, or to how many others, is another question, and one which we cannot answer, because no clinical records of the failures are kept.

The trend of scientific psychology away from introspection and self-analysis, and toward the emphasis on work and action, began many years ago. Its humorous expression had its setting at Princeton College, where the archway of one of the halls bears the famous Socratic inscription, in Greek letters, "Know thyself." Some shrewd wag, it is reported, drew a chalk line through this inscription and wrote beneath it: *Behave yourself*. This phrase epitomizes the findings of modern psychology that

21

a good personality or character is achieved by practice, not by introspection. Just as the pianist masters the intricacies of music through hours and years of practice, so the mastery of life is achieved by the ceaseless practice of the mechanics which make up the art of living. One hour of contemplation can furnish thoughts which weeks and months of action can scarcely achieve.

So a great cycle of human experience completes itself, and the life of Christ, with its conspicuous emphasis on good works, finds vindication 2000 years later in the developments of a science of human nature. The betterism, *behave yourself,* so far as its psychological significance goes, might just as well have been the New Testament saying: "Faith without works is dead."

However, I am getting ahead of my story, which is to tell how my experience with the problems of other people brought the truths of religion home to me. The cases which I shall present are naturally stripped of those personal details which would make identification possible. Many of them represent situations so common that they will identify themselves with people we know, maybe even with ourselves. They will illustrate the commonplace maladjustments of life, from which the more sensational maladjustments are bred.

One of these I remember vividly because of a peculiar telephone conversation. It was the case of a young woman, twenty-six years of age, unusually attractive on first acquaintance. The latter is important because the problem she stated was this: "I am worried because of the difficulty I have in making and keeping friends, particularly among men. I have met a number of men who seemed immediately interested in me and who invited me to go out with them. However, after the first or second invitation they just disappeared. I know this must be largely my fault, because when I am with them I feel myself unable to be interesting or to get them to talk freely. I have had an excellent secretarial position with the same firm for six years, so I can't be entirely stupid, but in this respect I am decidedly worried."

Going into detail, I found that she suffered this difficulty in making girl friends as acutely as in making friends among men. It also appeared that she disliked parties, danced but not well, disliked bridge, went to church but took no active part, knew some girls at the office but usually ate her luncheon alone. Very significant was her statement that most of the workers in her office, and most of the acquaintances in her family circle, were rather ordinary people, and quite beneath her intellectually and otherwise. Consequently she had very little to do with them and usually declined their invitations. Indeed, she met very few people she cared to become friendly with, but the trouble was that she was unable to become friendly with these few. Consequently, her opportunities for making friends were becoming increasingly rare.

My conclusions in this case will prove very disappointing to those who look invariably to the libido, a mother or father fixation, or an extensive inferiority complex as the explanation. This young woman had, for many years, done only the things she liked to do and avoided doing

23

those she disliked. This was the basis of her present difficulty. When her family friends gave the kind of a party she disliked, she either declined to go or, if she went, did not participate in the games or amusements which did not please her. When a young man whose education or literary interests were not equal or superior to her own asked her to go to the movies, she excused herself. For many reasons, and they were all logical from her point of view, she had cut herself off from the circle of people in which her social opportunities naturally lay. Consequently, she received fewer and fewer invitations.

My advice to her was to accept every invitation she received during the next six weeks and then report her experiences. I felt that the advice was perfectly safe in the circumstances. I explained that her inadequacy with people she liked was due to her failure to practice friendliness with people she did not like. Her problem was not one that could be solved by analysis and the searching for subconscious fears or inhibitions. I could not, by prolonged discussions, make her way suddenly easy. There was no psychological medicine or pill I could give her, no emotional appendix or tumor which I could remove. Just as she had to practice long and painfully to acquire skill in stenography, so she would have to acquire skill in making friends—accepting all the mistakes and embarrassments which this involved. No one could talk her into the acquisition of these skills. If she could act on my advice for the next six weeks, then I might help her further. If not, then there was little or nothing which psychology could do for her.

24

Three days later she called me on the telephone and asked: "Did you really mean that I should accept *any* invitation?" I replied: "Most decidedly, I meant just that. Why?" "Well," she said, "a young man has invited me to dinner and to the movies, and I don't think I ought to accept." "Why not?" I asked. "Is he a criminal? Has he been in jail? Does he mistreat his mother? Is he a gangster? Is he out of a job?" To these and a few more questions, the replies were all favorable. "Then, what is wrong with him?"

The explanation was that he was not very well educated, was not too perfect in his English, was only an auto mechanic, was a little uncouth. "Perfect!" was my response. "Suppose you try to make this young man's evening as pleasant for him as you can. Since you have nothing to lose, it should be easier for you to practice being a good companion. You are bound to learn something from this experience which will help you to be a better friend in the next. Call it self-sacrifice if you will, but the ability to make and to hold friends comes in no other way."

This instance is typical of hundreds in my experience, and in the experience of every observer. It illustrates the fact that a person cannot *choose* his friends until he has learned how to *make* friends. This young woman wanted superior friends because she considered herself superior, and in many respects she was superior; but in matters of friendship she was inferior. She had avoided the practice of friendliness with the people she thought beneath her, or the people she disliked. Consequently, she was unpre-

25

pared to win the friendship of the occasional person she liked.

The tragic side of this thoroughly selfish attitude and way of living is that the person's range of likes shrinks progressively, and his range of dislikes grows. How many times I have heard clients say: "Yes, I know quite a good many people but there are only a few with whom I care to associate much," and then give their excellent reasons. Seldom does a person in this state realize that the important point is not how few people he enjoys, but how many more he would enjoy if he made the necessary effort.

The person who exerts himself only with the people he likes, will develop more and more reasons to explain his dislikes for the people whose friendship he becomes increasingly incompetent to win. The habit of seeing the unworthiness of other people is usually a by-product of this inadequacy. The less able we are to deal with other people, the more we see to criticize in them. The former is a cause which we can correct. The latter is an excuse, no matter how logical or idealistic the words in which we phrase it. When our habits are wrong, our thoughts or explanations are bound to go wrong.

The problem, described by a man thirty-eight years old, was as follows: "I *have* a job which is driving me crazy. For ten years I have worked in a small department store as a sales clerk, window-trimmer, and general handy man. My employer is a greatly respected, successful man, but at times I loathe him. I hate the constant supervision under which I work. I have practically no responsibility or authority. My salary is fair, but I want to find a job in which I can become thoroughly absorbed, one which will give me a chance of self-expression and time to develop social connections. Also one which will enable me to leave this world a little better in some way for my having lived in it."

This man had no fault to find with his salary, but found a great many things to criticize about his position and his environment. For an hour he talked about the details of his life and work in a wholly reasonable manner, with only a few matter-of-fact questions interposed by me. At the end of the hour, my recording blank showed the following notes:

Single.

Lives alone, in rooming house, eats out.

Seldom sees members of his family—an older brother, two younger sisters, and a father living, all within visiting distance.

Indoor amusements, *reading*, mostly *good* books and magazines, for example *"Making Life Worth While"* by Fairbanks.

Doesn't like bridge or cards, tried ping pong once but gave up in disgust.

Evenings and Sundays, usually spent reading.

Sports, *none* either in high school or college (two years). Had no time for athletics, does not go to see games.

Church, Y.M.C.A., clubs, or social organizations, *none*.

Doesn't smoke or drink.

These notes represent a condensed history of this man's life in terms of what he had done and was doing. Whatever the causes, either in his environment or in himself, the keynote to his present predicament was the word "none." At one point, I find that I had jotted down his remark: "I seem to have had little time for outside affairs." His thoughts were to find work in which he "could become thoroughly absorbed." His behavior showed that he had become so absorbed in himself that it was next to impossible for him to become absorbed in any job or anybody. He had consistently done the things he liked to do and avoided the activities he disliked. He preferred reading about people to the effort of being with people. He enjoyed reading about the social system but avoided participation in its institutions. He studied treatises on self-improvement but shunned the most obvious activities which would bring it about. He wanted to make the world a little better, but he had shut himself off in a narrow world of his own, one which had little connection with the world at large.

A test of general intelligence showed that he was superior in this respect to 55 per cent of college students,[1] which placed him in the upper ten per cent of the total population, intellectually. A test of certain personality traits [2] gave the following results:

More introvert (and therefore more emotionally unstable) than 87 per cent of adult males.

More submissive or backward in social contacts than 81 per cent of adult males.

More self-sufficient or independent than 67 per cent of adult males.

[1] Otis Higher, Otis norms.
[2] Bernreuter Personality Inventory, Bernreuter norms.

The results of this test were quite in keeping with the habits of withdrawal from society, and the habits of self-analysis rather than self-discipline indicated by his way of life. His self-sufficiency and independence were adequate for the little world he had created for himself. About this test and its significance, especially in respect to introversion and extroversion, we shall speak more fully presently.

What could one advise a man in this situation? The most normal and wholesome element in his life was the position he already held. His problem was not a new and more absorbing position, but a different way of living, a greater turning outward or extroverting of his energies toward other people generally. He needed to spend his evenings in a pool room, or playing pinochle, or visiting with the publicans and sinners—even the most vulgar and wicked forms of social intercourse require some degree of self-denial and consideration for others. Better, of course, would be membership in a Y.M.C.A. or a church, or some political or social club in whose activities he might gradually find some wholesome absorption.

The obvious suggestion, according to a well known school of thought, would be that this man needed to get married and to raise a family. The importance of marriage and the proper sex adjustment has been recognized for centuries, but I am immediately reminded of many people who are not only married but happily married, and still unhappy with themselves.

One of them was a young college professor whose *only* satisfaction in life were his wife and two small

29

children. He defined his problem somewhat as follows: "I am finding it harder and harder to meet my classes. Often I must literally drive myself to class with all the will power I possess. When I get up before the students I am under a terrific tension. I feel nervous and irritable. I often lose my temper with some pupil over an unimportant trifle. Instead of laughing it off I blow up. I sense that the pupils do not respect me. Often my knees tremble and sometimes I break out in a cold sweat. It is all I can do to keep from running out of the classroom. At home when I should be concentrating on my studies, I think of these things, and then I can't concentrate."

Most of us have had all these experiences at one time or another, for example, at the thought of preparing and giving a public speech. They are quite normal occurrences which we manage to live through or conquer. In this instance they were becoming increasingly frequent and intense. The story of this man's life was much like that of the man previously described with two important differences. One, already mentioned, was his happy marriage. The other was the fact that he had made up his mind, early, to be a professor and had achieved the desired position while still comparatively young. However, in striving for this goal he had deliberately put out of his life every interfering activity. From his boyhood on, he had dodged all entangling alliances with other people. He had avoided indoor games and outdoor sports. He had joined no school societies, no clubs, no church. He had had no time and later no inclination to visit with other people. He had acquired no hobbies.

30

Now that he had achieved his goal, and a wife whose social habits were normal, he lacked the skills and practice necessary to pleasurable intercourse with other people. When his wife succeeded in getting him out or had people in, he suffered days of depression over his real or imagined social ineptitude. Consequently, these occasions had practically ceased.

As a refuge, he devoted more and more time to his studies and reading; but even these had lost their power to absorb his attention. He was finding it increasingly difficult to concentrate, and for long periods would just sit and think. Often he did not even think. When asked what he had done the night before, the night before that, and with his free time during the week including Sunday, the answer was usually: "Nothing," "sat around," or "discussed things with my wife," or "sat and thought." This man, in a test of personality traits [3] was found to be:

More introvert in his habits (and therefore more unstable emotionally) than 97 per cent of adult males.

More submissive or backward in habits of making social contacts than 94 per cent of adult males.

These test results were wholly in keeping with the history of his life and his present difficulties.

Many readers will naturally be curious about how such a situation can be dealt with, and I shall try to satisfy this curiosity, so far as practicable. However, the purpose of this book is not to describe the powers of

[3] Bernreuter Personality Inventory.

psychology, or a particular psychologist, in solving people's problems. Its object is to point out the conditions and the course of life which create these problems. How to avoid the unhappiness of a misshapen personality is certainly more important than the belated devices by which it can sometimes be remade.

Neither of the men just described was suffering from a temporary difficulty or from a nervous condition or breakdown as usually defined by the medical or psychiatric profession. Both were suffering the inevitable consequences of a lifetime neglect of many of the basic values of life. Whatever the causes—parental influence, an unfortunate environment, or their own deliberate actions—their failure to develop certain important habits of living had created for them a hell on earth. They were indeed reaping what they had sowed over a period of many years.

The frequency of cases like these, and the much greater frequency of similar cases of a milder nature, gradually forced into the forefront of my consciousness one of the great sayings of the New Testament: "He that findeth his life shall lose it: and he that loseth his life for my sake shall find it," [4] and again, "For whosoever will save his life shall lose it: and whosoever will lose his life for my sake shall find it." [5] The application of this great pronouncement to the cases just described is obvious. The common element in these cases was the fact that the individuals' governing principle in life had been

[4] Matthew 10:39.
[5] Matthew 16:25. See also Mark 8:35 and Luke 9:24.

to do those things they liked to do and avoid those they disliked doing. The result was that they liked to do less and less, and in the end, even the things they enjoyed most became as gall and wormwood.

"For my sake," for Christ's sake—this part of the principle raises a question. From a psychological point of view we may interpret this phrase as representing a set of values which transcend the values of the individual. Our personal inclination may be to do so-and-so, but some higher code, or ideal, or standard, or creed, leads us to sacrifice these inclinations and to follow the less pleasant, the more difficult course of action.

Asceticism, or the sacrifice of one's personal inclinations, is unquestionably the heart of the Christian religion and of all great religions. However, the principle of asceticism, applied to the details of living, leads to a fuller life, not to a sterile life. The sacrifice of immediate desires and inclinations for the performance of some less pleasant task, leads to a steady increase in the individual's range of interests, likes, and successes.

No discovery of modern psychology is, in my opinion, so important as its scientific proof of the necessity of self-sacrifice or discipline to self-realization and happiness. By nature, the individual is selfish, and inclined to follow his immediate impulses. The personality tests and the clinical experience of psychologists prove conclusively that this road leads to introversion, to emotional instability and neuroticism, to intellectual futility, to maladjustment, to unhappiness. It requires religion, or something higher than the individual or even a society of individ-

33

uals, to overcome the selfish impulses of the natural man and to lead him to a more successful and a fuller life.

Other interests, besides religion, often influence people to sacrifice their immediate pleasures for some more distant goal, but only religion embodies this principle as the major premise of a normal life in all its aspects.

The realization of this fact accounts, in large part, for my return to the church. I go to church, to repeat, because it has meant giving up things I like to do for things I did not like, at first, so well. I believe in God because I have found that without the belief in some one more important than themselves, people fail to achieve their own potential importance.

III

THE ACHIEVEMENT OF HAPPINESS

Verily, verily, I say unto thee, Except a man be born again, he cannot see the kingdom of God. JOHN 3:3.

It is the spirit that quickeneth; the flesh profiteth nothing. JOHN 6:63.

III

HAVING examined or given counsel to about three thousand individuals, I was reviewing one day the record of a man whom I had just interviewed. Suddenly it occurred to me: Here is the ideal type of the well-balanced individual, the unsung hero in a world of mental and moral conflict.

The man was without a job, he was not handsome, he was not brilliant intellectually or socially. He had only a few hundred dollars saved and in the bank. However, he possessed a collection of habits and beliefs which not only explained his present serenity, but were a guarantee of happiness in the years to come. All my experience with the problems of individuals, my first-hand statistical study of ten thousand cases already referred to, and my knowledge of the findings of other psychologists, contributed to this scientific intuition. Here are the notes I had jotted down to describe the significant facts about this man:

Age 28. Has been married two years.
Child, 6 months old.
Health: Reported excellent.
Appearance: Personable.
Education: One year of college, only fair in studies.

37

Favorite subjects: Mathematics, drawing, physics.

Religion: Baptist, member of church, teacher of Sunday School class at times. Liberal in doctrines but strong convictions of right and wrong.

Occupation: Unemployed. Had been manager of a retail chain grocery for four years and a clerk for three years before that. Chief ambition, engineering.

Occupational interests: Store work, mechanical engineering, and the tobacco business because of its importance in his home county.

Avocational interests: Baseball, basketball, and other competitive sports. Also dancing and card games.

Clubs and social activities: College fraternity, men's club in church, member of a rifle team.

Personality traits, as measured by the Bernreuter Test: Somewhat above the average in extroversion, emotional stability, self-sufficiency, and social ascendancy.

I am not a Baptist and I don't shoot a rifle, and it was not because of such specific details that this man's history impressed me. Rather, it was the entire collection of certain types of activities in his life which caused me to see him as an ideal type.

Contrast his record with that of the two men described in the previous chapter. They were employed. This man was not. They were miserable, emotionally unstable. This man, though worried about getting a job, was emotionally well balanced and basically happy. They were uncertain of themselves, and consequently of the world at large. He was reasonably certain of both, even though compelled to make an adjustment under the trying conditions of widespread unemployment. They lacked any definite set of beliefs or life values; they were adrift in the sea of their own logic. He was adrift in an economic chaos, but he was anchored to a deeper world and he was at peace with himself. Why this great difference between a man on the one hand so commonplace, so lacking in any noteworthy achievement, and the two men of considerably higher intellectual interests and attainments?

In technical psychological terms the answer would be that the two men were unusually introverted or self-centered, whereas this man was extroverted. He had developed habits and obligations embracing a much more representative range of life. In everyday language the explanation would be that the first two men had acquired predominantly *selfish* habits, whereas this man had cultivated *unselfish* habits.

Considerable confusion exists in the popular uses of the terms, extrovert and introvert, but essentially they mean degrees of selfishness, or the less selfish and the more selfish. The introvert or selfish person avoids the trouble of meeting people, the extrovert goes out of his way to meet them. The introvert evades the obligations and demands of clubs and committees, the extrovert accepts them. The introvert or selfish person may think of doing good deeds, the extrovert does them. The former has no time for the things he dislikes to do, the latter does them anyway. The former is afraid of making mistakes and of embarrassing himself; therefore he risks no action. The extrovert may be afraid, too, but still acts, and by his mistakes and suffering, ultimately achieves skill and confidence.

I have told hundreds of clients that it is better to make seven mistakes than to make only one. While one person hesitates because he feels inferior, the other is busy making mistakes and becoming superior. The introvert too often decides what to do or not to do according to how he will feel, the extrovert more often according to how his parents and friends will feel. The one reads about romance and adventure, the other uses his feet to find them. The introvert critically analyzes his friends and past experiences while the extrovert is making new friends and having new experiences. For the former, life becomes "sicklied o'er with the pale cast of thought"; the latter acts while his thoughts are still fresh. As a refuge from the hard facts of life, the introvert daydreams a world to his liking, in which he increasingly lives. When harsh necessity compels him to face certain situations, he cringes and suffers, he complains of an inferiority complex, he is unprepared.

This is the picture in black and white, and while many people fit these extremes, the majority are neither extremely introvert nor extrovert, neither wholly selfish nor unselfish. With them it is the direction of their development which is significant for their future happiness and success. Ten years from now, will they have grown more extrovert or more introvert? For extroversion and introversion are definitely habits which are largely within the individual's control.

Some people achieve extroversion by the development of a well balanced range of habits, from their childhood on. They may resemble the ideal type of man just described, not a great person nor a very successful person, but a happy one and a useful member of society. Some people fail to develop extrovert habits in their youth and are decidedly introvert at the age of twenty or thirty, and still achieve extroversion in later life. This happens only when the introvert succeeds in mastering some vocational pursuit which compels him to deal with people and which finally brings him recognition.

In a considerable number of instances which have come under my observation, I have seen artists, musicians, and professional people who were decidedly introvert, become more extrovert than the average person simply because of their concentration on developing the skills of their vocation. As they acquired these skills, they gained confidence in themselves and their ability to meet the situations in which their talents were useful. Incidentally, they were drawn into the stream of a wider social existence.

It is often said that the introvert is more sensitive to the finer values of life than the extrovert; that the great dreams and intellectual and artistic achievements of mankind are more likely to come from the former than the latter. There is absolutely no scientific evidence for this claim, and evidence is accumulating that the contrary is true. Recently I gave a test of personality traits to thirty successful and moderately successful artists, and they averaged considerably higher in extroversion than do people generally. We often hear that the artist is not so well balanced emotionally than the average individual, that he is and should be given to temperamental outbursts. This test showed that the contrary was true, and that success-ful artists were better balanced emotionally than most people.

Obviously, the musician who practices six hours a day, who must fit his performance into the exacting require-ments of an orchestra and an audience, who must persist in his efforts in the face of discouragement and often ridicule, is bound to become more extrovert and to ac-quire habits of emotional equanimity. The artists who remain introverts are usually those who fail to sacrifice their pleasures and impulses to the strenuous demands of practice and competition. Their aspirations remain dreams and fantasies and as such benefit neither them-selves nor humanity.

Usually, however, extroversion is achieved by develop-ing a well balanced set of normal habits. A young engi-neering student was brought to me by his parents because he was having unexpected difficulties with his studies. Standard tests which I gave him indicated that his intel-lectual capacities were more than equal to the require-ments of the school. Probing further, I found that he was also having great difficulty getting along with the boys in the fine fraternity to which he had recently been elected —in fact, he was seriously thinking of withdrawing from the fraternity entirely.

I asked him what the favorite activities of his frater-nity brothers were, and some were not admirable but others were quite harmless. Ping pong and bridge were two of the chief amusements.

"What do you do," I inquired, "when the boys ask you

to play ping pong?" "I excuse myself by telling them I am a rotten player, and," he added vehemently, "I am rotten." "Then you probably go to your room," I told him, "and start to study. After a few minutes of concentration you suddenly find yourself thinking about ping pong, and how awkward you are at it, and how unpleasant it was to have to refuse the invitation in that way, but how much worse it would have been if you had accepted, and yet what a good time the boys will be having. Then you try to get your mind back on your work, but soon the laughter and shouts of the players reach you, and off you go again with regrets and excuses for yourself. The more you think, the worse you feel, and the harder it is to concentrate on your studies. In an hour's time you accomplish what fifteen minutes of complete concentration would have done."

Yes, that was the story, he admitted. "But what should I do?" he wondered. "Play rotten ping pong," I told him. "Play it with good players if they ask you; drag out some one as poor as you when they don't; make up your mind to suffer, but no matter what happens, play. Before long, you may find some one who plays worse than you do. Later you will find yourself winning a few points from a better player. Soon you will find some pleasure in just trying to play, and after a twenty-minute bout will go back to your studies without the gnawing regrets that raise such havoc with concentration. Having expended this energy in a popular activity with some degree of satisfaction, it will not rise to plague you in your next undertaking."

43

Ping pong, after all, is a trivial part of a college career, and yet no college education is complete without it or its equivalents in the amenities of life. I advised this young man, already unable to get good marks, to study less and to play more. Having failed to acquire an adequate collection of play and social habits, sufficient at least to meet some of the requirements of his environment, he was not only miserable in his fraternity, but unable to concentrate his really good mind on his studies.

He could, of course, have withdrawn from the fraternity and isolated himself with students of his own kind. The quickest and easiest way to solve emotional conflicts is to avoid their causes, to withdraw from the realities of life, to narrow one's circle. Such a solution is bound to be temporary, and to result in the shrinking of the individual still further. It represents the process of introversion which, if continued, leads to still greater emotional upheavals later on. This boy was already insufficiently extroverted and too unstable emotionally. It was high time that he began to face life, and to develop habits with which to meet it more successfully.

To him, as to many engineering students, I was able to explain introversion and its resulting emotional upheavals by a very simple mechanical analogy. When the energies which the body creates are carried off smoothly by various sets of habits which produce satisfying results, then a person is extroverted and consequently serene or well poised emotionally. However, when the necessary habits are lacking, the human organism is like an automobile engine racing out of gear, or with gears

44

clashing. The engine wastes power turning over on itself without getting anywhere, or it moves in fits and jerks as gears are clumsily engaged.

All people are emotionally upset at times, due to this cause. When we meet a person and don't know what to say, or say the wrong thing, we get red or feel embarrassed. There is an excess of unexpressed energy or of energy awkwardly expressed. Such emotional irritations are to be expected by every normal being, and are helpful in so far as they stimulate him to develop better habits or greater skill. They reach the point of harmful emotional unrest when a person accepts defeat, ceases to try, and therefore fails to acquire a sufficient variety of habits or skills to meet the common situations of life adequately.

This is not the only cause of neuroticism or emotional unrest, of excessive worry and periods of enervating depression, but it is probably the most common. Few people suffer from an excessive expenditure of their energies, but multitudes suffer from surplus energies which remain unexpressed or are expressed in ways that are not normal. The selfish person is the person who hoards his energies and suffers, finally, from their excess. The unselfish person expends his energies lavishly in many directions, thereby leaving little surplus energy to feed the gnawing demon of discontent.

One of the controversial doctrines of the New Testament is that expressed in John 3:3. Jesus talking to Nicodemus, says: "Except a man be born again he cannot see the kingdom of God," and (John 3:6) "That which is born of the flesh is flesh; and that which is born of the Spirit is spirit." The doctrine of original sin and the emphasis on the rebirth of the individual, has often been a vexing one. The studies of psychologists throw an important light on this doctrine. From a psychological viewpoint, we are all born as introverts, and as selfish individuals. We achieve extroversion or unselfishness only by a continuous process of rebirth, the painful birth of new habits and new personality traits. In early childhood, many habits are acquired unconsciously and through the insistence of parents; but soon they must be acquired by conscious and often painful effort.

The child is born into the world as a bundle of unorganized energies. It is a power-producing machine or organism which sleeps, is fed, and creates energy but has no habits by which to transform this energy into useful actions. Everything must be done for it, it can do nothing for itself. It waves its arms but cannot direct them; it wriggles its body but doesn't get anywhere; it moves its eyes but cannot focus them. Gradually it acquires the habit of grasping objects, of focusing its eyes, of crawling, of walking, talking, running, eating, dressing itself, going to school, reading, writing, saying the multiplication table, etc., etc. All these acts represent habit patterns by which the child is enabled, more and more, to transform his natural energies, his three meals a day and his night's sleep, into actions which absorb these energies. This is the a, b, c, in the process of extroversion.

After about six years of daily practice, often painful to both parents and child, he has mastered the habits of eating with a knife and fork sufficiently to avoid embarrassment in company. In less time, possibly, he has learned to say *please* and *thank you*. In time he acquires habits of getting along with other children, of avoiding quarrels, of making friends and acquaintances. He learns how to play games, often develops proficiency in one or more competitive sports or amusements. He may acquire habits of doing work around the house, of doing his school home work, of visiting friends and inviting them to his home, of going to Sunday School or church. He may develop hobbies, the habit of collecting stamps, of practicing on some musical instrument, of building radio sets.

All such habits and many others represent the process of extroversion, of turning one's energies *inside out* into actions that provide satisfactory contacts with an ever expanding world. From the world of a mother's breast to the world of an adoring family; the world of parental *do*'s and *don't*'s; of visitors; of neighbors' quarrelsome children; the school; the city; the realm of books, movies and the radio; the field of games and sports, and social intercourse generally; the college; the job; courtship, marriage and the responsibilities of a family; all the thousands of habits developed to meet these situations represent the process of extroversion, the process of being born again.

The young man described as an ideal type had acquired a comprehensive set of habits dealing with a variety of common situations. He had not acquired these habits or skills without many sacrifices of his momentary inclinations. Often, when he felt like sitting comfortably at home with a book he had gone to his club because it was club night. Many times when he felt like going to the movies he had accepted an invitation to play bridge instead. Frequently, when he felt just like talking with a friend, he had torn himself away for strenuous baseball or basketball practice. Many of the pursuits he now enjoyed or took for granted had once made him miserable because of his awkwardness or lack of skill.

He had been actuated by external and religious ideals which transcended and often interfered with his own pleasures or aims. Why had he not finished college, I asked him. Because he had felt that his family needed his support more than he needed the education. Did he like to teach Sunday School? Yes and no. He liked the boys but it was an effort to prepare the lesson and get up on time Sunday mornings.

The introverts we have described developed their lives according to an opposite principle, a principle widely described as *self-expression*. They had done what they felt like doing when they felt like it. They had failed to practice the many habits which lead to skill and satisfaction in a variety of contacts with people. They had pleased themselves first and so failed to learn how to give themselves to others. They had devoted their energies to the narrow subject, themselves. Now their energies were eating them up. They were finding that oneself, as an object of attention, is not sufficient for success; that doing the things they liked and avoiding those they disliked, led to a sense of inferiority and an emotional

48

hell. In trying to find their lives in their own way, they had lost them.

There is, of course, the danger of acquiring too wide a range of skills and activities, of being too highly extrovert. Concentration on a vocation or a career must always be the unifying core of a personality. However, the danger of over-extroversion is far more remote than the danger of excessive introversion. Extroversion is the result of work, a life of practice. Introversion is the result of avoiding practice. The extrovert suffers more in the beginning. The introvert suffers more in the end.

Jesus Christ, the ideal of unselfishness and the great exponent of the unselfish life, was an extrovert. He was extrovert to a degree which few can hope to achieve. He was highly aggressive in making social contacts. He did not hesitate to accept water from the woman at the well because she was a Samaritan, nor did he refrain from talking with her because she was ignorant and did not speak his language. He did not confine his attentions to those who were worthy of him but devoted himself to Zaccheus, the tax-collector, Nicodemus, the Pharisee, to the halt, the maimed, and the blind, the publicans, and the sinners. He did not wait for people to invite him, he invited them. To Peter and Andrew, casting their nets into the sea, he said: "Follow me, and I will make you fishers of men." He sent his disciples and the seventy out into the world to carry his message. Before sending them, he gave them a course of training in how to approach people. He preached meekness in spirit but boldness in action.

49

Although inspired by the concept of a higher life, his own life on earth was a series of intensive and extensive social contacts. While trying to motivate people for their ultimate good, he was much more conscious than his disciples and others of their immediate physical needs. He was quick to see others' points of view, even though he had positive ideas of his own. The intrusion of little children did not upset him, the pressure of the multitudes did not embarrass him. Instead of avoiding the people whose mode of life he criticized, he visited them in their homes. His energies and inspiration were being constantly converted into useful deeds and contacts with a wide variety of people. He went up into the mountain to pray, but he was, above all, a man of action. He believed in principles, but he practiced them in living, and he lived an abundant life.

The extrovert or unselfish character of Christ was not an accident. It was the result of an ideal which he valued more highly than his personal comfort or even his life. "My meat is to do the will of him that sent me," he said. His acts were motivated by an idea and a conviction far more powerful than the physical and moral obstacles which obstructed him. He knew nothing of the glands regulating personality or the inherited bodily structure which medical enthusiasts now say make one man inevitably schizoid, another cycloid, and others paranoid or epileptoid. "I can of mine own self do nothing," he said; "as I hear I judge: and my judgment is just, because I seek not mine own will, but the will of the Father which hath sent me." And whether it was to attend a wedding in

Galilee or to take up his cross in Gethsemane, his governing principle was the same:

"Father, if thou be willing, remove this cup from me: nevertheless, not my will, but thine be done." This was Christ's principle of living which, in essence, is the psychological criterion of an active, out-flowing, and a happy life.

IV

FOOLS OF REASON

I am the way, the truth, and the life. JOHN 14:6.

Now faith is the substance of things hoped for, the evidence of things not seen. HEBREWS 11:1.

Whosoever shall not receive the kingdom of God as a little child shall in no wise enter therein. LUKE 18:17.

IV

BECAUSE so many people have asked me to be their god, I have come to appreciate the significance of a real God. To some extent this is the experience of every psychologist, physician, or clergyman to whom people bring their deeper problems—that is, unless he be a prig wholly lost in his own conceit.

One of my most poignant experiences was that with a man who had just been released from prison after serving a sentence of twenty years for the murder of his wife's lover. His excuse for coming to me, as he expressed it, was:

"I want to find out whether the many years I spent in jail have affected my mind or unfitted me for a job. So that you will know the facts, I will tell you that I was a stationary engineer, and always had a steady job. This man broke up my home, and I deliberately shot him. That one act was the only bad act of my life. I never smoked, drank, or gambled. My conduct in prison was such that I was paroled four years before my sentence was up.

"While in prison, I did everything I could in my spare time to keep my mind occupied. I studied French and German especially, and I can read and speak both languages now, though my accent is not very good. [Here he demonstrated his knowledge.] I knew that to keep myself from becoming peculiar in that place I must study something regularly.

"I have $80 in addition to the twenty-five which they gave me when I left. All of it I saved from the postage stamp allowance which we got every week. My wife died two years after I was sentenced, and I had no one else to write to, so instead of spending my stamp money on tobacco and candy, I saved it.

"Now I want to get a job as stationary engineer if I can, but I am worried. What if, in spite of my efforts to keep my mind balanced, the years in jail have made me peculiar without my knowing it? That's why I came to you, to find out if I am all right."

As well as I could, with such tests as were available, I reassured him, but felt pitifully inadequate in the process. Here he was, trying to start life again in the midst of wide-spread unemployment, and with the added handicap of his crime and prison record. He needed far more than the professional reassurance of his mental capacity. He needed a set of beliefs and convictions far superior to the practices and prejudices of society. He needed a tower of strength infinitely more stable than the logic of his own mind, however well balanced.

And yet, this ex-prisoner was better balanced, emotionally, more extrovert in his habits, more aggressive socially, than many of my clients, or than many people one meets every day. Some individuals have so imprisoned themselves and their energies as to be virtually

56

doomed to a life of solitary confinement. They walk the streets, they do their work, they speak when spoken to. They are often cultured and converse brilliantly on the subject which interests them. Nevertheless, they tread in endless circles the narrow cell of a self-centered mind. With a devastating logic, they have destroyed every belief or conviction which might serve them as a means of escape.

An extreme but not unusual example is the case of a man who believed in nothing at all. This man, highly introverted by lifelong habits of withdrawal from experience, was finding it increasingly difficult to carry on his job or to follow any of the simple pursuits of a normal life.

"Naturally," he said, "I have given this a great deal of thought, and I have read widely in scientific books on psychology to gain an insight into my situation and an understanding of what I should do. However, every process of reasoning leads me to just one conclusion: Why do anything? Why should I even make an effort to teach my classes? I have no evidence that the subject I am teaching is doing them more good than harm. For all I can be sure of, I am wasting their time and they are wasting mine. And assuming that my courses are important, somebody else could give them as well, probably better than I can.

"Why should I associate more with other people? Why should I join a Y.M.C.A.? For every set of reasons favoring some course of action I find just as many reasons against it, and just as good reasons. Then why

57

do anything? Why make the effort? Even my family would probably get along better without me than with me.

"Now you will probably recommend that I do certain things for my own good. In advance, I know that I shall question your reasons, and probably conclude that there is just as logical a case against doing what you recommend as is the case you will make out."

Here was an instance of the complete triumph of reason, almost pure reason, over the emotions, beliefs, prejudices, and automatic or unreasoned habits of life. Without employing any shams or trickery, I was compelled to answer this man as follows: "I agree with you perfectly and, lest you believe that my agreement is only a matter of tact, let me illustrate with a homely habit which is hardly ever questioned by adults.

"Why should we eat with a knife and a fork? Using knives and forks is an absolutely unreasonable habit. It means extra work in setting the table, extra work in clearing, in washing and polishing the silver. It provides one more source of infection by germs from other people. Knives and forks cost money in the first place. They cost parents about six years of irritating effort in training their children to use them properly, effort which might well have been put into higher things or saved entirely. How much simpler and more natural it would be to eat with one's hands and fingers, the tools nature has provided!

"You can make a similar case against any other phase of life, and so can any intelligent person. I certainly

58

shall not argue with you, or try to convince you by reason. All I can do is to ask you one question: Are you satisfied with your present existence? This is not a question of logic but one of feeling. Do you want to remain as you now are? If your answer is, Yes, then there is no way in which I can help you. If your answer is, No, then I may be able to help you and you may be able to help yourself. Then for example, I can say that eating with a knife and fork is right, not because it is the only logical way to eat but because you will feel better among other people if you are using a knife and fork as skillfully as they are. Then I can suggest other things for you to do, which you will do not because they are logically defensible, but because, as you do them and become more skillful, your satisfaction will increase."

The state of mind just described is one common to introverts who have learned to substitute thinking for action, reason for faith, analysis for conviction. It is particularly characteristic of very good minds, minds which are well read and educated. One of the most brilliant boys I ever examined, who was having difficulty in making passing grades when he should have been at the top of the class, wrote his father a perfectly logical indictment of a college education. Most parents and friends have had the baffling experience of trying to convince, by reason, some one who reasoned as well or better. Their reasoning may be perfect, yet we know that they are wrong.

A famous French psychologist conducts a sanatorium for extreme introverts, or successful extroverts whose minds have become tired and disorganized through too much use. He works with them somewhat as follows: To begin with, the person must have sufficient faith in him to agree to do as he is told, without asking questions. As soon as the patient disobeys or questions an order, he is dismissed. This psychologist may take a client to a field and point to a fifty-foot strip of land, three feet wide, which has been staked out. He then hands the client a pick and shovel and tells him to dig a ditch to the depth of his own height. Each day, with an increasing number of hours up to a maximum of ten, the client must labor at this ditch. When the fifty-foot ditch has been dug and the psychologist has passed on its satisfactory completion, he tells his client: Now fill it up again. A sufficient number of unreasonable tasks like this often restores reason to its proper balance in the sum-total of personality, and often turns a person's energies outward and away from himself.

Fortunate indeed are the men who persist in knocking a little white ball around in every direction except the right one; who have a lawn in which the weeds, despite their continual efforts, never stop growing. Fortunate the women with families whose appetites are never satisfied long; who, in spite of their chores at home, must still sew with the ladies' auxiliary. Fortunate all those people who, through either choice or force, make the most of the unreasonable tasks of living, whether they be digging ditches or scrubbing floors, collecting postage stamps or crocheting doilies, driving a truck or washing the baby's diapers.

60

Among the philosophers and scientists there have always been some who maintained that life was not a logical or rational experience and that nature could never be explained in terms of scientific knowledge. Individuals are born for no reason of their own. They live by a mixture of instinct and reason which is neither rational nor consistent. They die with a capricious certainty entirely beyond their logic to justify. The mind is neither capable of solving nor intended to solve these problems. Reason is not an end in itself but a tool for the individual to use in adjusting himself to the values and purposes of living which are beyond reason. Just as the teeth are intended to chew *with,* not to chew themselves, so the mind is intended to think *with,* not to worry about. The mind is an instrument to live with, not to live for.

And yet, there can be no questioning the fact that Western civilization for centuries has deified the mind and reason as an end in itself. Our pursuit of scientific knowledge and the trend of our entire educational system has been a glorification of intellect and a corresponding disintegration of the basic values which make intellect worth having.

There are signs in every field of an awakening to this great fallacy. However, it has remained for psychologists to discover how damaging to the individual's happiness and success a too great reliance on thinking may become. Both through their experiences with individuals and through scientific tests on groups of hundreds of thousands, the broad implications of this discovery are being revealed—in relation to education, religion, personality, and the philosophy of life generally.

There can be no solution of life's deeper problems, no increased happiness for the individual, through the development of greater scientific knowledge alone. More science only adds more confusion. Unless the sciences are integrated and subordinated to the homely facts of everyday living, they will destroy rather than liberate the minds which created them. This integration must come from without the sciences themselves, it is not inherent in them and it is not a subject for scientific proof. It must come from a faith, a belief in certain values of life which is fundamental and which no logic can displace.

This sounds complicated in theory but is simple in actual experience. The young man who could find no reason for doing anything, in the last analysis, found that he did not want to remain as he was, and this desire proved stronger than all his logic. Children are compelled to do many things which seem to them unreasonable for no other reason than their parent's command.

A striking line from one of Ibsen's plays, uttered in a moment of emotional stress, has never escaped me. "Without a fixed point outside myself," exclaims one of the characters, "I cannot exist!" What infantile nonsense! was my reaction at the time, since I had just been studying the history of philosophy and the so-called foibles of the unsophisticated mind. What fixed point is there outside oneself, and who but a weakling needs such a crutch? Since then, I have listened to the same cry from hundreds of individuals, uttered in many different forms,—the cry for a vocational objective, the cry for an objective in life, the cry for release from intellectual and emotional conflict, the cry of those for whom life had turned sour.

Psychologically, and in fact from every conceivable point of view, the individual seems made to believe, and to act on faith. Agnosticism is an intellectual disease, and faith in fallacies is better than no faith at all. How well I remember my highly intellectual scorn for people who believed in numerology and astrology, in palmistry and phrenology, in spiritualism and mental telepathy, in Couéism and New Thoughtism, and the many other fads and theories which the facts of science either definitely disprove or cast serious doubt upon. I now see that such foolish beliefs are better than no beliefs at all.

The belief in palmistry leads, at least, to the holding of hands; phrenology to the study of other people's heads; numerology and astrology to an interest in people's birthdays; spiritualism to the joining of knees under a common table. All such beliefs take the individual out of himself and propel him into a world of greater interests. Incidentally, it is a significant phenomenon that so many great scientific minds have failed to find satisfaction in the science in which they were really competent and have turned to the study of mental telepathy or spiritualism for comfort.

How chimerical and empty are such beliefs as compared with the belief in religion, which affects life in all its aspects and the essential details of which no science can disprove! The idolatry of reason and the intellectual scorn of religion has rendered man prey to the innumerable quacks, pseudo-scientific fads, and political panaceas which bedevil him today. How far more rational, if rational grounds were needed, is the belief in prayer, in immortality, in the Lord's Supper, in the Divinity of Christ, and other moot questions about religion, than the fantastic beliefs men grasp at today! The belief in God, in the Ten Commandments, and the teachings of Jesus is certainly less open to controversy than most pseudo-scientific cults with which men drug themselves. It is not only natural for man to believe in something—it is absolutely essential; but in the absence of an irrational belief in religion, he becomes the fool of every faith which promises the abundant life *as he, at that moment, desires it.*

Observing the fad psychology of our age, the commandment: "I am the Lord, thy God. Thou shalt have no other gods before me," assumes a new and a terrible significance.

For some years now, psychologists have been making scientific studies of the psychology of beliefs and their relation to life. Tests of various kinds have been developed for use with individuals and with groups, such as the Allport Scale of Values, embracing religious, social, aesthetic, and economic beliefs; the Thurstone Attitude Scales, of which there are seventeen applying to religious beliefs, racial beliefs, economic beliefs, etc.; the Doll Maturity Scale, and many others. Nation-wide studies of the changing trends in people's beliefs have been made with increasing frequency.

One pertinent study in this field is that bearing on unemployment relief. A group of about fifty psychologists and their students made nation-wide tests in fifty cities with the question: Do you believe that your city, your state, or the Federal Government should take care of unemployment relief? The results, reported by Dr. Paul S. Achilles, in the Proceedings of the American Psychological Association at Ann Arbor, in September, 1935, were as follows:

Answers, including some who named more than one	Feb. 1933	April 1935	May 1935
City	43.4%	25.4%	17.7%
State	25.9	24.9	21.5
Federal Gov't	33.4	39.8	47.9
Don't know	15.5	18.7	21.1

These results show a remarkable trend away from the belief that the city and local agencies should help the unemployed, and toward the belief that the Federal Government should be responsible.

The escape from a personal and moral obligation which this trend represents could occur only in a society which lacked religious convictions and principles in the first place. The faith in a vicarious agency which this trend indicates can mean only the absence of any genuine faith of individuals in themselves and their obligations. Like the disciples who wanted to send the hungry multitude elsewhere, the voters hope to escape responsibility for the unemployed.

65

We see here a national tendency toward introversion, and in the light of events, a nation of people following the apparently easy way, dodging the realities of life, avoiding personal contacts with suffering, and missing the first-hand experiences with people which lead to extroversion, competence, and an abundant life, for themselves as well as the unemployed. We see, in short, the adoption of an apparently reasonable program which, in effect, is an intellectual excuse for avoiding what is right. We place the god of reason, or of political expedience, above the stern God of Duty. The more intellectual the man, the wider his range of ideas, the more danger he is in of putting gods of temporary expedience before the God of everlasting values.

As a psychologist, I shall advise, and as a man, I shall try to help, those in need; but I refuse to be God and I hope to avoid depriving any individual of his birthright to independence, to first-hand experience, to suffering, and to such happiness as his own efforts may bring. I am reminded of one of my cases, a fine aristocratic-looking Scotchwoman who was in a state of turmoil. She was about fifty years old, was passing through the climacteric, and another still more disturbing experience. Her husband, just succeeding in business, had died leaving her with a daughter five years old, and practically no income. Her family, though cultured, was poor, and so she emigrated to America and entered domestic service. At the time of her visit to me she had for ten years been the housekeeper in a wealthy family, with from ten to fifteen servants under her supervision. She looked and evidently was a very capable woman.

Her daughter had married a man against her wishes, and although she had tried to leave the couple to themselves, their difficulties had made it impossible. After buying a house and establishing a scale of living equal to their income, the husband had lost his position. The situation was complicated by the birth of a child. The mother felt compelled to aid the young couple from the savings of twenty years, and the demands had increased until her funds were almost gone.

From the first, the couple had quarrelled and the husband had been extremely jealous, and the arrival of the child had increased rather than diminished their differences. The details of their quarrels, as related to me, were most harrowing. On one occasion, the wife was barely saved from an attempt at suicide. Later, she fell in love with a neighbor, the father of four children, who was equally enamoured of her, but would do everything except give up his family. During the past month she had been seriously ill, and the doctor had advised a few months of complete rest and change of scene, involving another heavy call on the mother's funds and even the necessity of her taking temporary leave from her position to be with the daughter and her child.

"What have I done wrong and what can I do now?" cried this poor woman. "I don't know where to turn or what to do next! Always I have been deeply religious and prayed for guidance, but the last few years have shaken even my faith in God. I know I have made mistakes. It might have been better if I had denied them financial assistance from the first. Then at least they would have given up their house and this latest complication with another man would have been avoided. But what shall I do now, or after my daughter recovers? One of the men you have helped and who noticed my distraction, urged me to see you, and while I had had little faith in such things, he finally persuaded me to come. Is there anything you can do to help me, anything you can tell me?"

What could I tell her? What could anybody tell her? The emotional dangers of the climacteric—she had mentioned this herself. The emotional involvements of a lone woman with her only child? She had acknowledged them. The mistakes of too generous financial assistance? She regretted them and was no longer able to repeat them. Who could foresee or deal confidently with the developments of this situation?

What this poor woman needed was strength not criticism, assurance not condemnation. What I told her was: There is only one serious mistake which I can see that you may possibly make, and that is losing your faith in God and your religion. Your religion does not promise you a perfect life on earth, nor freedom from suffering; it does guarantee you the strength to bear suffering. Your religion does not expect you to be free from sin or mistakes in judgment; it does promise you forgiveness for your mistakes. Your religion expects you to continue making the best efforts you can on behalf of others; it does not guarantee that you or anyone can arrange the lives of people as he pleases.

Above all, your religion means a trust in God and his sometimes mysterious ways. Such trust will give you the inner security and confidence you need to carry you through this difficult situation. I may make a few helpful suggestions in this matter, but no human being can give you anything comparable to what your religion will give you. You are infinitely fortunate to have a religion to depend on.

I am glad to say that this woman had no further need for me. Subsequently, I learned of the serenity and the new confidence with which she had assumed her cross and was doing the best she could in a situation where she, more than any other person, was concerned.

Religion has been called the refuge of weak minds. Psychologically, the weakness lies rather in the failure of minds to recognize the weakness of all minds. With all the developments of modern science, with all the general and higher education peculiar to the United States, and with all the mechanical aids to understanding and intelligence supplied by our means of rapid communication, the nation is floundering as it never has done before. There have in the past been conflicts over slavery, states' rights, free silver, the tariff, prohibition, and other issues from time to time. Now there are conflicts over innumerable issues all at once, most of them centering around mathematical and mechanical schemes for a more abundant economic life.

Many of these schemes have been proposed by the

shining lights of our intellectual age. Their exponents have in common one pervading characteristic, namely, an unbounded intellectual arrogance, in which a supercilious contempt for the simple and basic values of human nature is coupled with a fatuous faith in the omnipotence of their ambitious plans. The fact that the plans of one contradict the plans of another is inevitable when minds have cast loose their anchors to beliefs and traditions more basic than their reason.

The more we know the less we know: the less we know of the basic values of life and of character, which are religious, often unreasonable, and in the last analysis, beyond reason. The mind, coupled to religion, is a stronger mind for it, a mind not so readily swayed by the passions that parade as reason under an enlarged vocabulary. But in deifying the mind we have abandoned God. We have become the fools of reason and the dupes of scientific truth. As Aldous Huxley has said it, "Ye shall know the truth and the truth shall make ye mad."

V

WINE AT WEDDINGS

*And the third day there was a marriage in Cana of Galilee. . . .
Jesus saith unto them, Fill the waterpots with water. And they
filled them up to the brim. And he saith unto them, Draw out
now, and bear unto the governor of the feast.* JOHN 2:1, 7, 8.

V

WINE AT WEDDINGS

JESUS not only attended the wedding at Cana, but when the conventional wine gave out, he was amenable to his mother's suggestion that he help the party by producing some wine artificially. Jesus is not commonly thought of as a social light, and yet the story of his life is a story of winning friends of all kinds in all kinds of situations. He was forever changing the water of existence into the wine of social intercourse.

From a psychological viewpoint, all friendship involves an artificial process, namely the process of subordinating one's own interests and inclinations to those of others. People who have acquired the art of friendship no longer think of it as artificial. For them it is natural, or second nature, to say and do the things which please others. Indeed, they may even think that they are pleasing themselves, rather than their friends. They are, because to give pleasure to others has come to be their own first principle of enjoyment.

The miracle of friendship becomes most obvious in the case of people who have not learned the mechanisms of unselfishness, or the habits of giving themselves up to the activities which other people prefer.

On Playing Bridge

People have said to me: "No, I don't play bridge. I consider it a waste of time." Others have said: "Yes, I play bridge, but I hate to play with people who take it seriously." Yet I have recommended to hundreds of clients that they learn to play bridge or that they take it more seriously, on the ground that bridge is one of the most fruitful disciplines in acquiring unselfish habits and desirable personality traits.

The person who does not like to play bridge seriously is one who doesn't like to be reproved if he trumps his partner's ace, ignores his partner's discard, fails to return his partner's lead, or forgets what is trump. As one of four players, three of whom have acquired habits of paying attention to the bidding and each other's playing behavior, the casual player is likely to say such things as: "Oh, is it my turn to bid?" or, "I didn't hear what the bidding was"; or when the bidding is completed, "Now what is trumps?" When he picks up his hand he may say: "Let's have a new deal, this hand is terrible," and during play his thoughtless remarks will reveal the position of cards which will give the opposing pair unearned tricks.

In short, such a person is thoroughly selfish in his disregard for the pleasure of three people. He lacks the habits, and sometimes even the desire, of paying strict attention to the acts and remarks of his co-players. He insults them by saying, in effect: Your concentration and pleasure in this game is silly. Why don't you take it

74

lightly *as I do?* A person who lacks the sensitive habits of tact or considerateness in bridge, probably lacks them in other social activities. If he plays bridge at all, he should take it at least as seriously as the people with whom he is likely to play.

Learning bridge involves the acquisition of a whole collection of definite extrovert habits—I have counted fifty-three and there are more—of paying attention to other people and their acts. I have recommended the game particularly to introverts lacking in social charm and effective social techniques. If such a person learns to play a fair game of bridge, it means first of all the concentration of his mind on something outside himself, something that gives many other people considerable pleasure. Being able to play the game gives him a wider opportunity to meet people on a common ground. If his game is acceptable, the fact that he is not a brilliant conversationalist will not be so embarrassing to him. In such favorable circumstances, the acquisition of collateral social graces is made easier.

I hold no brief for those who consider bridge a matter of life and death, or for those to whom bridge is an end in itself. But as a discipline in unselfish social habits and as a tonic for an able intellect, it ranks high in the category of worth-while human activities.

Children should be taught to play bridge at an early age. They may not like it. The process may involve compulsion. A father and mother, asking their two children to sit down to a game with them, may be met by the remark: "I want to listen to the radio." When this issue has been settled, the children may play in a spirit of silliness, and with a deliberate lack of attention or cooperation. Soon they will want to stop. Then it behooves the parents to say: "If you will give the next four hands your complete attention, you may stop. If not, we shall play another four hands."

A year later, one of the children may come home from an evening's visit at a friend's house and say: "What do you think? We played bridge and my partner and I made a grand slam!" From being an effort and a bore, bridge has become a pleasure, a step in the building of a more effective personality, an achievement in the techniques of social cooperation—indeed a step in the direction of greater peace and harmony among the nations. Few human activities require such meticulous attention to the rules of good behavior as does bridge.

On Dancing

In my religious upbringing, cards, dancing, and the theater were taboo. Yet I find nothing in the teachings of Christ, nor in the Bible anywhere, to justify the rigorous attitude which the churches once had and some still have in respect to such pursuits. Almost any activity, no matter what its merits, may become a source of evil or a snare of the devil. Dancing has great merit, and I have recommended it to literally hundreds of clients.

The following situation is typical. A man twenty-six years old, a decidedly pleasant-looking individual, with a remarkably good position, has become so unhappy that he is seriously considering suicide. He proves, upon examination, to be extremely self-centered, and lacking in friends and social contacts. Most of his evenings are spent in reading. Among other things it appears that he has no friends whatsoever among women, never invites a girl to go anywhere with him, and avoids as poison all affairs at which women are likely to be present. This, of course, is only one aspect of his problem, but an important one.

Often, in such cases, a man would be told: You need a woman. In all my experience, I have never told a man he needed a woman or a woman that she needed a man. In hundreds of cases, however, I have made practical suggestions leading to the development of habits and activities such as would make a client a more fit companion for members of the opposite sex. Bridge, for example, is one such activity. Dancing, however, is one of the quickest and most wholesome psycho-therapeutic devices for reducing the artificial barrier which often develops between members of the opposite sex.

My remarks on this aspect of the young man's problem were somewhat as follows: The world of people is divided into two parts, men and women. By your failure to develop certain basic habits in youth, you have entirely eliminated from your life the female half of the world. Every person's natural energies, as a human being, are such that a very considerable part of them can find satisfying expression only in the female half of the world. Expressed normally, these energies would take the form of chatting with girls in school, going to parties

77

at which girls are present, the many activities of court-ship, and finally marriage.

Marriage and parenthood represent the high point in the expression of one's natural energies in relation to the opposite sex. However, because of the very nature of these energies and the physical intimacies which they involve, people, in youth, often acquire a fear of physi-cal contact with members of the opposite sex. They build up a physical barrier so rigid and so active as to make even the most casual physical contacts abhorrent. A boy may read romantic novels and enjoy the most fervent scenes, but merely to shake hands formally with a real girl is a most painful experience, one to be avoided at all costs. The consciousness of this barrier poisons all natural and casual meetings with women. Even to talk with them is more difficult than talking with men. Women, just because they are women, are an alien race.

The value of taking dancing lessons is that it com-pels a man to make physical contact, not with one woman but with many women. He finds that it is not so terrible nor so difficult as he had imagined. Moreover, in the concentration of trying to adjust his steps to those of his partner, he begins to appreciate that here is a coöpera-tive activity in which two people must strive for perfec-tion, both subordinating themselves to the discipline of an imposed rhythm. He finds that he must adjust himself to different partners, say different things, try different steps.

In short, he finds not woman, but women. He comes to see that women are people and not so terrible or

78

difficult as he had thought. He has taken a long step in the direction of expressing his energies in that half of the world for which so large a share of his energies was by nature intended.

This is a subject about which I prefer to talk less and do more. The importance which it has assumed in recent years has been too much in the nature of an intellectual and conversational *chef d'oeuvre* and not in the nature of practicing normal activities, of which dancing is one. Dancing, like most other social activities, requires the acquisition of many unselfish habits. I have told many clients that, in their quest for happiness, they would do better to use their heads less and their feet more.

On the Successful Business Man

The business man, the employer, performs daily the miracle of converting water into wine. He converts raw materials into the means of a livelihood, and he converts undirected employees, individualists, into members of a team which has both direction and power.

The religious concept of unselfishness is often interpreted as a form of weakness, self-effacement, and self-denial. The unselfishness of Jesus, no matter how we interpret his sayings, did not take these forms. His life was a series of good works, his unselfishness consisted of doing things with and for other people. Extroversion, or the psychological definition of unselfishness, implies action, not passivity. Indeed, the studies of psychologists prove quite conclusively that the most highly extrovert individuals, as groups, are the successful executives and business men, the men who have built up their own fortunes, the doctors, lawyers, or professional men and women who have won a wide clientele, the artists who have achieved recognition for their work, the inventor who manages to get his devices accepted.

In these days of calumny and invective, it is difficult to speak of successful business men as highly unselfish. The passions of people impel them to think of selfishness in terms of possessions. Those who have must be selfish; those who have not must be less selfish. The reverse is often true. Psychologically, the wealth achieved by a successful business man is not so important as the habits by which his wealth was achieved. Psychologically, we know also that the successful employer is nearly always less self-centered and possessed of a wider range of unselfish habits than are most of his employees. He is often not as well educated or as intelligent scholastically as many of his subordinates, but he is usually equipped with a much wider range of habits for dealing with people *as they like to be dealt with* than are his employees.

The employer who assumes the responsibility of giving work to other people, of providing the necessary weekly payroll, of entrusting larger responsibilities to his subordinates as the business grows, of meeting the risks of competition, labor problems, manufacturing difficulties, and the thousand and one griefs that go with almost every business, manifests daily a high order of unselfishness. Through his energy and leadership, he

80

improves the lot of his employees far beyond the point which their personal efforts would have made possible. The fact that he may benefit, materially, more than any other one individual, is inevitable in the situation and not an indictment of his character.

That some employers are more generous and progressive than others does not alter the fact that both kinds are more unselfish and more extroverted than the rank and file of their employees. They not only are usually able to take care of themselves but will often be found to be taking care of many other people less able and more selfish than themselves. When they come to me as clients it is usually in behalf of their children or friends.

Indeed, the very essence of business success lies in the degree to which an employer, in competition with others, can benefit both his employees and his customers. Competition between people in business, as in every other field of human relationships, is a great stimulant leading to the practice and the acquisition of skills and habits of consideration for other people. Many individuals remain employees rather than employers, day workers rather than executives, because they have been unable to sacrifice their selfish desires or their personal ease to the acquisition of the skills and resources which make for success. They have not learned how to confer enough benefits on their fellow men to warrant positions of trust and responsibility.

These remarks are prompted by the frequency with which my young clients have resented the exigencies of a business career or the ideals of what they designate often as mere money-grubbing. Again and again I have found daughters and sons, incompetent and uncertain themselves, yet highly critical of a father whose business or professional success has provided them with unusual opportunities for education and growth. They resent especially his ideals and suggestions for their own welfare, and regard him as narrow-minded and old-fashioned, even as selfish. They are totally unable to appreciate the homely values and disciplines by which his competence, or competence in any field, is achieved.

To a Student Waiter

DEAR FRANK:

Your account of your experiences waiting on table came back to me after you had left. I couldn't help but realize what a significant job this might be in the development of personality and active charm.

You might be interested to learn that to a considerable number of my clients I have recommended getting a job as a sales-person in a department store, for no other reason than the effect it would have in developing certain desirable personality traits. "In such a job," I told them, "you will be compelled all day long to listen to customers, to pay close attention to their minutest signs of approval and disapproval, to anticipate their desires, to please them in every possible way that will lead to a sale or to their coming back to you again. You will develop habits of concentration on other people and their wants, habits of subordinating your own likes and dislikes, of saying and doing the things that please. Such habits will stand you in good stead no matter what you do later. When you can please even those customers who are unreasonable and downright nasty, then you will have won a great victory over yourself and added a wonderful weapon to your battery of social charms." I have, as a matter of fact, had clients who were unbelievably benefited by following this advice.

Waiting on table is a very similar job, and even though you are doing it unusually well already, or think you are, it has possibilities and refinements far beyond those which any person can master in only a few weeks. All depends on how you approach the job. If you regard it merely as a chore, to be gotten through with as easily as possible, you won't develop far. If you can see it as an opportunity for practicing alertness, anticipation of people's wants, suggestions which might please them, then you can make a high art of waiting on table.

I am not suggesting subservience or the sacrifice of dignity. There is nothing inconsistent with the preservation of your self-respect or social equality and the development of skill as a waiter. It is only the person who resents the job and its requests for service who puts himself in a position of becoming subservient. You can be just as dignified and superior being a waiter as can the master who sits at the head of the table or the rich classmate who commands your attention—more so even than the latter.

Maybe you remember the story of how Jesus washed his disciples' feet and answered to their protests: "Ye call me Master and Lord: and ye say well; for so I am. If I then, your Lord and Master, have washed your feet; ye also ought to wash one another's feet." Nowhere, probably, was Christ's inner dignity and superiority so conspicuous as in this lowly act.

You can learn to serve people so well, and make such an exciting game of your job, that you will be remembered long as a waiter par excellence. Such an approach to your task will result in making it a source of great pleasure and pride.

You spoke about losing the school social hour through this job. You are, as a matter of fact, gaining the opportunity to prepare yourself for the most profitable social hour you can possibly have, if you develop a technique of serving your tables and even those within the reach of your attention in a way which will command their admiration.

So, my dear Frank, I hope that you will not look too longingly after a different job which you think now would be better. Try to look at this situation with vision, the vision that includes the development of active charm, as achieved through unselfish service.

On Converting Good Books

"I don't care about reading trash, but read only such books as will improve my mind and my knowledge of good literature. Here is the list of books I have read in the past two years." With this remark, a young woman gave me a typewritten list of about one hundred and fifty books. It was an admirable list of good biographies, novels and essays, and I complimented her selections highly.

"How many people have you become acquainted with in the past few years?" I inquired. This question gave her considerable difficulty, for she could hardly name five new people with whom she had exchanged more than casual greetings. I found that she had just finished a year's college course in the study of personality, and she showed me her elaborate notebook, containing many charts by which she and the other members of the class had rated themselves on various personality traits. "How many members were there in this class?" I asked. "Thirty-seven, and well over one half of them were men," she informed me. "Did you discuss any of the subjects with members of the class after or before the study period?" She explained that she usually arrived just in time for the lecture and left immediately at its close, so that she had had no opportunity to do this.

One of the things she had learned from her classroom studies was to smile more often, since a cheerful smile had been rated as one of the most effective elements in an attractive personality. As she talked with me, with almost clock-like regularity her mouth widened and her teeth appeared. It was a swift and automatic grimace, without trace of mirth or happiness. I had not the heart to speak of it or to discuss, in this specific connection, the basic satisfactions which make a natural smile inevitable.

As tactfully as I could, under these difficult circumstances, I explained to her the difficulties of developing a good personality in a vacuum. I advised her to join a Y.W.C.A. and to become involved in its group and social activities, to take a more active part in the work of her church, to join a dancing class. I suggested that she give up entirely the reading of all books of any kind for a year and confine her reading entirely to the *New Yorker* magazine, the *Reader's Digest*, a chapter each day in the Bible, and a daily newspaper. The money she had been spending on studies and consultations in regard to her personality I advised her to spend on clothes and her personal appearance, and on activities involving her contacts with other people.

This woman was typical of many people who believe

85

that they can improve their personalities by intellectual concentration on themselves. Actually, the process works like the mind of a woman sitting at her dressing table, looking at her face in the mirror. She sees a flaw in her skin and looks more closely. She moves her face still closer to the mirror and examines the blemish more carefully. She takes her hand mirror and gets close to the light, so as to get the best possible view. The longer she looks and the closer she looks the worse the blemish appears, until finally she is convinced that she looks like a hag and has one foot in the grave. Whereas if she were out with a group of people, probably not one in ten would even notice the blemish that disturbed her so much.

On Religious Conflicts

The problem stated by a woman thirty-seven years old and unmarried was as follows: "I have a great deal of leisure time and no financial worries. My family owns a department store and wanted me to work in the store, but it seemed to me that with so much money in the family, it behooved me to do something more worthwhile. Consequently, I became a part-time worker in several charitable organizations. However, I have found these activities less and less satisfying as time went on. They seemed somehow to lack reality, and to leave me uncertain of the importance of the work I was doing.

"My discontent has been aggravated in recent years

by the feeling of hypocrisy that overwhelms me while observing certain church rituals, especially the Communion. I have always been a church member and I believe in religion, but I cannot accept literally all its forms. I do not believe, for example, in the literal interpretation of the words, 'This is my blood' and 'This is my body,' and when I am participating in the rite, I feel as though I were doing something terribly wrong. During the past year I have been taking a course in psychology and one in religion at a theological seminary to help me in resolving this conflict. I cannot say that these courses have helped me."

This problem, as stated, lends itself readily to the obvious psycho-analytic interpretation. Quite likely, if this woman had found a career in marriage, her religious conflict would not have arisen or become so troublesome. However, what had hindered her marriage and what was she to do now? In the first place, she had failed to throw herself wholeheartedly into the work she undertook in preference to a business career. While despising the business which made her free choice possible, she was unwilling to make as complete a sacrifice of herself in charity work as the business man or woman has to make in a business career. She had played at being a charity worker, and because she failed to take the work seriously, it came in time to seem to her unreal, unsatisfying. Since she did not give it all her energies, it in turn failed to give her all its satisfactions, either in friendships or worthwhile achievement.

On the contrary, she was left with much spare time and energy which, lacking in satisfying outlets, encouraged self-analysis, day dreaming, and random activity, all of which were conducive to the development of emotional conflicts. Her trouble with religion was but one result. If, in accordance with the teachings of Jesus, she had led a life of intense and self-sacrificing activity, the minor details of religion would never have become an all-absorbing preoccupation. She might either have found some good man and married him, or have been able to sublimate her frustrations as a woman on some satisfying plane of activity.

Now, I could only recommend facing the facts and making the attempt to start in a career involving genuine pressure from without. In my notes on this case I find the following: Religious conflict and what it implies will never be solved by intellectual considerations. Situation calls for a minimum of self-analysis and of analysis by others. Primary corrective is undertaking a real job, possibly beginning as a saleswoman in family's store. Such a pursuit will give mind an objective outside itself, needed above all. Such a job will give power over *things* which, in turn, will lead to power over *people,* which again, will lead to *self-confidence.* Such absorption will place many present conflicts in a better perspective, thus reducing their magnitude and simplifying their solution. If wages are an obstacle, give the money to charity. The working for definite wages, however, will give work a reality lacking in previous activities.

On Character and Personality

A body of educators is now in the midst of an extensive study on the relationship between education and character. Its findings should prove to be interesting at least to the extent of raising more vividly the question of the difference between character and personality. The two words may be used synonymously if we are agreed that they mean the same thing and also what they mean. Often, however, they are used to mean different things.

When people say that a man has a good character, they frequently mean that he is honest, does not steal, is true to his word, is steady in his habits. He may nevertheless be a dull and ineffective individual and quite lacking in what we mean when we say that a man has a good personality.

In so far as psychologists can define "personality" in a sentence, there would be rather general agreement on this: Personality is the extent to which the individual has learned to convert his energies into habits or actions which successfully influence other people. A homely girl who can play the piano entertainingly has a better personality than a homely girl who cannot. An awkward, unattractive boy who has developed skill at tennis, becomes more attractive in motion, and his ability at tennis brings him friends he would otherwise not have. The man or woman who has acquired the skillful habits of entertaining or helping people need not worry much about being an Adonis or Venus.

The compound of acquired skills, both in play and in

89

work, constitutes personality, and gives the individual the power to attract and influence others. How often clients have said to me: "If people don't like me for what I am rather than for what I can do, then, I'd rather not have them like me at all"! This attitude shows a failure to understand the nature of personality. A person may be charming as a picture, but a picture is not a personality except when in motion, except for what it does.

For these reasons, psychologists have defined personality traits thus far in terms of extroversion, social ascendancy, self-sufficiency, emotional stability, and similar habit patterns. Whatever the terminology or the tests used, the units of measurement are acquired habits or attitudes representing collections of habits. Honesty as such is an extremely difficult trait to measure, though in so far as it represents an active regard for the rights of others, it runs through all extrovert habits. Industry is a difficult trait to measure, though in so far as a person has learned to convert his energies through many useful habits he is more industrious than the person who hoards his energies.

It may truly be said that even in this sense there have been fine personalities or characters without the influence of religion. Even though true, the question still unanswered is this: What basic principles or values help most in the achievement of personality? We shall probably all agree that the great pagan personalities of history were dominated by some goal or ideal which lifted them far out of themselves and which approached, in its compelling drive, the supernatural beliefs of religion.

90

VI

CHILDREN ARE MADE

Now no chastening for the present seemeth to be joyous, but grievous: nevertheless, afterward it yieldeth the peaceable fruit of righteousness unto them which are exercised thereby. Wherefore, lift up the hands which hang down and the feeble knees; and make straight paths for your feet, lest that which is lame be turned out of the way. HEBR. 12:11-13.

VI

CHILDREN ARE MADE

VIVIDLY do I remember a hot September afternoon, returning on the train from Forest Hills where my wife and I had been watching the tennis matches. Somehow, we got to the subject of children attending Sunday School. The question in our minds was whether or not we should send our children, then four and two years old, to Sunday School. My wife and I had been compelled to attend not only Sunday School but church, regularly, from our very early childhood on. In our occasional revolts we had been met by the stern insistence of deeply religious parents. Their religious discipline had included our not infrequent accompanying them to week-night prayer meeting, our attendance at classes for the study of the catechism, and our presence in later childhood at many other church functions such as the Young People's Society, and periodic series of revival meetings. At home we had learned to say grace at all meals, and had been required to participate in family devotions at which we all took turns reading from the Bible and then knelt while the head of the family led us in prayer.

Upon entering college, this discipline was automatically left behind. Except for the college chapel service, of pleasant variety, no formal religious observance was required. Not only did we receive freedom from religious routine, but the education we received gradually emancipated us from the intellectual routines of religion. We learned, in the light of modern science, how absurd much of the Bible was. The religious doubts which we had expressed before coming to college, and which had been dismissed by our elders with brief explanations, now received major consideration. Indeed, many of the elements of religion which we might never have questioned, were brought under the microscope of scientific or historical research, and there transformed into the squirmings and writhings of little minds.

In the end, we had learned that the concrete details of religion, the Church and the churches, the creeds and the doctrines, the rituals, the ministry, the regimentation of people in religious practices—all these were but the superstitious mistakes of uninformed minds trying to express the spiritual core of religion.

There was left then, of religion, that abstract core, a God stripped of any concrete characteristics or any definite connection with the world of our daily behavior or the institutions in which we had been reared. This was called a *spiritual* conception of God. Actually, it was a scientific abstraction, a purely intellectual concept similar to that reached by the physicist in his analysis of matter. Starting from the tangible and solid facts of matter and substance, the physicist, by way of the elements, the atoms, the molecules, the ether squirts, finally reaches the ultimate abstraction: Matter consists of *mass*

94

points in motion. Beginning with much that matters, the physicist ends with something that matters little or nothing.

So we and many others, beginning with a substantial if not altogether comfortable heritage of religious habits and practices, were aided to arrive at a concept of God as an abstract something, maybe The Mass Point in Motion. Some pupils were so apt in this process of abstracting the anthropomorphic and material elements from religion that, in the end, nothing believable was left. They became, like many of their teachers, complete sceptics or agnostics. Others, however, were so stupid, so impervious to the meaning of the courses they were studying, that they went right on believing the untenable doctrines and routines they had acquired in childhood. I should say, with a high probability of accuracy, that the emancipation of students from religious doctrines was in almost direct ratio to their I.Q., or intelligence quotient. The greater their intellectual capacity, the more quickly they saw the absurdities of religion.

My wife in one of the great colleges for women, and I in one of the renowned colleges for men, received the Phi Beta Kappa keys. We both profited by our education to such an extent that we became virtual agnostics. If we believed in God at all, it was the most vague and attenuated kind of belief. Certainly it had nothing to do with the Church, the practices and preachings of which had by this time become repugnant to us. We considered ourselves above such antics.

On that hot September afternoon, on the Long Island

95

suburban train, we came to this broad-minded conclusion: We would neither discourage nor encourage our children to go to Sunday School, but would let them make their own free choice. We would not repeat the duress to which we had been subjected by our parents. We would let our children be guided by their own intelligence, and if they wanted to go to Sunday School, they could go. We were both well pleased with this decision, which was so in keeping with our modern and enlightened times and the so-called new psychology of self-expression.

We were only one of many young couples at that time making virtually the same decision. Again and again, our conversations with other parents would lead up to a statement on their part like this:

We are not sending our children to Sunday School or Church until they are old enough to know better, or old enough to know what it is all about. But what troubles us is whether they will acquire the strong sense of right and wrong, the definite moral beliefs, which we acquired in our childhood. We were taught that certain things were right and wrong because God or the Bible said so. The method may have been primitive, but the effects were certainly good. At least, we learned a great deal about right and wrong living. Now we can only tell our children that certain acts are good or bad because *we* say so, or society says so. Is that as strong? Will it be as effective? Will our children, without the pressure of religious doctrine, acquire the basic moral values of life which we

96

automatically accept, even though we no longer accept their divine origin?

I cannot begin to remember the many times and the many ways in which this question was discussed by parents with a religious heritage and a modern education. I only know that we were beginning to feel the responsibilities of parenthood, and that we were unprepared to answer this question. Whatever the answers we devised, I have since learned that they were wrong, and wrong from every psychological, philosophical, and common-sense point of view.

The rearing of children is a task of such magnitude, one so intricate in its complexities and so baffling in its contradictions, that parents usually need every iota of help they can obtain. It was only natural, having dispensed with the aids of religious beliefs and institutions, that enlightened parents should turn to other sources for help, and where more naturally than to the psychology of childhood? The psychology of childhood was not ready for them. The science had progressed only to the point of confidence in theories. Scientific evidence was still very meager, though theories were plentiful.

Parents accepted the theories, among which were such as these: that corporal punishment was psychologically harmful; that a child should be reasoned with rather than dogmatically coerced; that the child should not be repressed—on the contrary, it should be allowed to express itself; that left-handedness was an inherited mechanism; that a child was born with a certain I.Q. or level of intelligence and nothing could change it; that children should be given a regular allowance in order that they might learn the value of money; that some children were naturally nervous or sensitive and should therefore not be compelled to do what other children do.

None of these theories was ever substantiated by scientific psychological evidence, and practically all of them have been proved definitely erroneous. Left-handedness is not inherited but acquired by the accidents of early training. Physical punishment, orthodox child psychologists now agree, is not only permissible but at times the most effective way of dealing with a child and much less injurious than prolonged reasoning and discussion. Arbitrarily enforced commands by the parents and the lessons of unquestioned authority are considered an indispensable element in the rearing of a child. The I.Q. is not an infallible measure of the child's intellectual capacity, but only a rough measure of what the child will do in the field of orthodox education. Moreover, when the I.Q. is measured, the good or bad influences of training and environment have already distorted the result so that the intelligence quotient of young children of intellectual parents may be 1.50 whereas five or ten years later it may be down to 1.25 or even 1.00. A regular allowance may give children some idea of money's value but is just as likely to encourage their habits of getting more and more for nothing. The over-emphasis on expression, fostered by the movement for progressive education, we now have learned leads to mental and moral chaos. Self-expression is desirable, but only in its proper place. That place is defined by the discipline and conventional habits which make it possible for people to live together with a degree of harmony.

For the past three years I have been experimenting with the development of a test for children between the ages of ten and eighteen, a test calculated to measure certain personality traits or habits somewhat after the order of similar tests devised by psychologists for use with adults. The traits measured by this test are:

Extroversion, or habits of paying attention to other people and their interests, and habits of developing skills and competence in certain activities.
Social ascendancy, or habits of taking the initiative in meeting and dealing with people.
Self-determination, or habits of subordinating impulsive tendencies to a more distant goal.
Economic self-determination, or habits of doing work for the sake of money or some objective that costs money.
Sex adjustment, or habits of meeting and dealing with members of the opposite sex.

This test has now been given to 2000 children and undergone an elaborate process of checking and statistical analysis. Its results show that among the most important habits contributing to an effective personality are the following:

Going to Sunday School and having parents who attend church. The children tested who had these characteristics were much more likely to rank as extrovert and socially ascendant than the children who did not. The very fact of parents attending church was a factor in the development of desirable personality traits on the part

99

of their children, and the attendance of Sunday School by the children was an even more important factor.

Having served on a committee or committees; belonging to a club, school society, orchestra, Boy Scouts, dramatic society, etc.; attending school affairs like athletic events, parties, plays and recitals; children who did these things were more likely to be extrovert and socially ascendant than were those children who did not.

Children who often do things they don't like to do simply because they think they should do them; who like to try things even when they can't do them well; who, when they know they are not good at something take special pains to improve; who, when they have two things to do, one they like and one they dislike, generally do first the thing they dislike; who often do things they dislike because it will help them to realize some ambition; children with these habits and tendencies are much more likely to rank high in extroversion and self-determination than those who lack them.

Contrariwise, children who often say: I can't do this or I am no good at this; who often lose patience with themselves and give up trying to do something because they are awkward or embarrassed; who often refuse to play games because they lack skill; are much more likely to be introvert and socially submissive.

Among the habits contributing most heavily toward introversion, social submissiveness, and dependence, are: losing one's temper frequently; getting blue or sulking when things don't go to suit; exaggerating and fussing about ordinary incidents; not being a cheerful loser; having hard luck or brooding over mistakes. All these items represent habit mechanisms which, as they become fixed, prevent the child from acquiring many desirable habits and personality traits. They are among the principal sources of emotional unbalance and inferiority, just as the other habits mentioned above are the sources of superiority and emotional stability.

The habit of criticizing or finding fault with other people; of interrupting conversation; of saying right out what is on one's mind rather than restraining this impulse for fear of hurting people's feelings; these habits are very important factors in producing a socially submissive personality and a personality that is supersensitive to criticisms by other people.

Contrariwise, the child who often pays compliments or says things which he knows will please other people; who tries to be friendly with all people whether he likes them or not; who has learned to control his feelings so that people won't know he is boiling inside; this child tends to rate high in personality traits and is not so easily upset by the criticisms of other people.

The child who usually goes to sleep promptly after going to bed is likely to have a better personality than the one who lies awake thinking. The child who is often fagged out during the day so that he doesn't feel like doing anything is more likely to rate as introvert. These findings should be considered together with the following: that children who participate in many games and sports, and especially those who are practicing consistently in a few sports, or who participate in competitive atnletics and games, tend to stand much higher in personality traits than those who do not.

Children who like mathematics and the sciences, including the mechanical and household arts, tend to have better personality traits than do the children who prefer English, languages, and history.

The fact that children get an allowance from their parents, have a savings account and save money, is found to have no bearing on their personality traits in either direction. Children, however, who sell tickets, do chores, and go out to get jobs doing things they don't like in order to earn money, are far more likely to have desirable personality traits than the children who never do these things.

Finally, there is no relationship between the standing of the children in respect to the personality traits measured by this test and their standing in their studies or in a so-called general intelligence test. Other psychologists have also found that there is no correlation between scholastic success and a good personality.

Tests like the above, and the analysis of the habits which contribute to a good personality, represent the attempt of psychologists to do what the field of education has never done—that is, to codify the habits and elements which go to make an effective personality. Education has codified arithmetic, spelling, reading, and all the various subjects which are supposed to develop a good mind. There are hundreds of subjects, and thousands of textbooks, many kinds of courses and curricula, representing the structure and codification of intellectual learning. It is a magnificent structure from the standpoint of size, detail, and comprehensiveness. But nothing like it exists in the field of personality and its development.

Minds are not born, they are acquired by training. Personality is not born, it is developed by practice. But we have no library of scientific books on the latter. The greatest and most authentic textbook on personality is still the Bible, and the discoveries which psychologists have made tend to confirm rather than to contradict the codification of personality found there. Psychology differs from all other sciences in this important respect. Whereas the other sciences have taught us that our previous ideas and beliefs about nature were wrong, psychology is proving that many of the ancient ideas and precepts about the development of a good character and personality were right.

The keynote which runs through the elements or habits of personality included in this test is this: The child develops a good personality, or at least the foundations of such a personality, by doing many things which he does not do naturally, and many things which he actually dislikes. Eating with a knife and a fork may become natural to him in time, and even enjoyable, but not until his parents have spent four to eight years of laborious effort in getting him to use them properly. Children vary, of course, by nature and heredity; but no matter how good they are, the basic habits must be inculcated by a process of discipline. In view of the inevitable resentment toward discipline which children develop and their inertia in acquiring many desirable habits, every available influence, pressure, or device which will hasten their acquisition of these habits must be utilized. Most parents need every source of help or support available in this process.

From a psychological as well as from a common-sense point of view, the greatest source of help is religion. The religious belief in God, the Ten Commandments, and the teachings of Jesus, gives parents a certainty and an authority with their children which they otherwise lack. Those parents who wondered how, in the absence of the religious influences which had moulded them, they could mould the moral habits of their children, were facing an unanswerable problem. There is no rational substitute for the supernatural power which the unquestioned belief in a Divine Being and a Divine moral order confers.

Parents who have been emancipated by education and reason from this belief are uncertain themselves. How then can they be authorities to their children? In the absence of religious authority, each parent must become an intellectual and often an original authority on the many questions of right and wrong, good and bad habits, which he is trying to impress upon his children.

The older the child grows, and the more he comes under the influence of the conflicting authorities of society—the school, the neighbors, the gang, the town—the more difficult the task becomes. Indeed, it is an impossible task, and the confusion in the minds of so many parents these days is eloquent testimony to the truth of this statement.

Religion is the only unifying and ever-present force

which can help to solve the inevitable moral and intellectual conflicts of parents, children and society at large.
In a world of change and rebellion to authority, God is
the only fixed point.

The child upon whom the existence of God, as a supreme arbiter of good and evil, has been impressed early
in life, has already acquired the basic motive in developing good habits. The basis for his actions, instead of
being one of likes and dislikes, becomes one of right
and wrong. He might like to disobey his mother but he
knows that it is wrong. He might not like to return all the
change from a purchase, but he knows that it is right.
He might not like to be unselfish with his playmates, but
he knows that he should. Naturally, the process is not so
simple as this; but the habit of differentiating between
selfish, personal impulses and a more important good,
between pleasure and duty in short, is fostered.

The doctrine of original sin, and the conquest of the
natural man, so important in religion, is profoundly true
from a psychological point of view. The habits of a good
personality are acquired by the conquest of laziness and
natural impulse. In so far as religion impresses this upon
the child, in terms of the many good habits which he
must learn, it hastens his acquisition of good personality
traits.

Many parents have told me that their children were
just naturally lazy. No doubt some are, and often due
to natural causes. But industry and energy are acquired
habits no matter what the physique. The more skills and
mechanisms the child develops, the more readily such

physical energies as he may have translate themselves into action.

Many parents have told me that their children are naturally nervous and given to loss of temper. Again, these natural tendencies are converted into more wholesome directions to the extent that skills in games and work are acquired. The teachings of religion in regard to sin, the conquest of the natural man, the necessity of the continuous rebirth of the individual, have their maximum value in the malleable years of the child's life.

The Sunday School and the Church, whatever their shortcomings as institutions, do help to inculcate the basic concepts of right and wrong, selfish and unselfish action, in the growing child. They help to establish the basic belief in God and a divine moral order as the source of these concepts. They are, therefore, of incalculable assistance to parents and society in giving children the necessary foundation for developing good characters and personalities. It is not surprising that the test described above should show that children who went to Sunday School had better personality traits than those who did not, and that children of parents who went to Church had better personalities than the children of parents who did not go to Church.

In the study of 10,000 adults already referred to, it was found that those who belonged or went to a church had significantly better personality traits than those who did not.

The theme of personality development outlined here is not one of self-suppression but one of self-expression.

106

The mere suppression of the natural impulses, of an explosive temper, for instance, is psychologically inadequate. The over-emphasis on "Thou shalt not" is undoubtedly harmful. Even so, there must be in the training of a child a certain amount of direct and uncompromising repression. However, the positive side of personality consists of expression, of learning to do an increasing number of desirable things well.

Expression, as I define it, consists of substituting for the less desirable acts and habits others which are more desirable.

The fallacy underlying the progressive education movement is that it has not codified the forms of expression which are desirable and those which are not. It has assumed, too uncritically, that what a child wanted to express was worth encouraging. It has made a god of the principle of expression at the expense of the manner of self-expression. Consequently it has often confused self-expression with self-indulgence, dawdling, and a set of adult notions about the framework—art, dramatics, pageants, etc.—in which children should self-express themselves. It has failed to recognize sufficiently that mature self-expression and creativeness rest on the acquisition of the basic techniques of self-expression, just as the mastery of a piece of music rests on the mastery of the scales.

The child compelled to practice the piano and certain exercises against his will is acquiring the a, b, c's of musical expression. The child allowed to practice as he pleases, to draw pictures as he pleases, and to follow other pursuits with a wide latitude of action, is usually wasting the time in which he might be mastering the basic routines. The enforced practice of many desirable habits of expression, such as those suggested in the test described, automatically widens the range of worth-while self-expression later on.

Here are some excerpts from a letter such as any father might write to a sixteen-year-old son:

DEAR SON:

If I were to be asked what is the dominating motive in your life, that is either the strongest influence or that which appears most frequently, I should say it was the desire for fun, to have a good time. There are all kinds of fun, such as competitive sports, cards, swimming, reading, just fooling around, the movies, etc., etc. But if I were asked to define what you considered fun, it would be: doing just as *you* please.

In short, your idea of fun, as I have seen you over a good many years, is to do just *what you want to do when you want to do it.* That is to say, fun with you is a matter of impulse, likes and dislikes at the moment, and almost entirely without a plan.

Now fun, and having a good time, may be wholly worth while and an important part of a person's development, but only if it is guided by certain more important considerations. Fun only on impulse, or fun which consists of doing just what you like to do when you feel like it, is absolutely ruinous to the development of an effective personality. In addition, it kills off, one by one, the activities which a person can enjoy, so that the older he gets the less fun he can have.

Take tennis, for example. Until recently, tennis was fun only when you felt like playing, or could play without too much trouble, or with someone who was not too good, or who, even

108

though a good player, liked you well enough to put up with your game. The more your game improves, the more people you will enjoy playing with and they with you. It will become an increasing source of enjoyment and friendship as the years go on, both with boys and with girls. But in order to improve your game, so as to get more and more fun out of it, it is absolutely necessary to play it on many occasions when you don't feel like it, or when you would much rather be fooling around with a friend doing something else. You must work for it, you must talk for it, plan for it, play with people you don't enjoy or who don't enjoy you; in short you must make yourself go through a certain amount of hell for the time being. To have fun at tennis, it isn't necessary to become an expert. It is necessary to develop a degree of relative superiority so that you will be increasingly welcomed as a partner by an increasing number of people.

The radio and the movies are two of your chief pleasures. Both of them have merit, but the more time you spend listening to the radio or watching movies, the less time you have to practice the things you should be learning now. Merely watching other people perform will not make you a performer. If you denied yourself these passive pleasures more, and exerted yourself in systematic practice at tennis, art, hockey, music, with which you are now dabbling, you could have much more fun next year, and every year after.

You have some examples already in your own experience. You have had a great deal of fun out of your musical instruments, but your fun was in playing them the way you wanted to play instead of in practicing and the drudgery of mastering music. Consequently, you are having less fun from this source as time goes on and as you find yourself stacked up against people who, possibly with less native talent, have sacrificed some of their fun to painful practicing. The same thing will happen with your talent and enjoyment of art, unless you take it more seriously. In other words, you can't draw or practice

109

when you feel like it or when it is fun, only, and expect either to get anywhere or to retain your pleasure in it.

At present, you are making a fine effort to get ready for the examinations, and really subordinating many of your fun impulses, quite seriously, to this end. Remember, you are now paying the price for the fun you had, or thought you were having, on the many occasions in the past when you should have been studying.

Even now you have plenty of time for fun and for just fooling around, but your idea of fun, as you told me to-day, is sitting around if you feel like it, and in general, doing what you feel like doing. That kind of fun won't get you anywhere and will ruin your fun next year and in later years.

You have often complained about my unsympathetic attitude toward your desire to have some fun. You miss the point. I am not against your having a good time. In fact, I believe that right now you are not getting nearly enough fun out of life. You don't have nearly as many good times as you should be having. The reason I have insisted on your working at certain jobs is not to keep you from having fun but to keep you from wasting your time on the self-indulgence which you consider fun, and to prevent you from falling entirely into the habit of doing just as you please. If you had put your mind and energies to the systematic cultivation of superiority in your studies, in your art, in certain competitive sports, in your social contacts and in social games, I would not be nearly so insistent on your doing certain chores around the house.

I believe that you are smart enough to see the simple logic in this situation, and to realize that what you have been calling fun is too often the poison of self-indulgence. You have shown many signs of the power to control your impulses and to reconstruct your habits. Your recent tendency to play more tennis is such a sign. I believe that your next big step, and probably the most important one that you will ever take in your life, is to

110

change your concept of fun from acts based on impulse to fun based on a plan.

Incidentally, the amount of fun you have is determined not only by how competent you become through practice, but also by how much pleasure and satisfaction you can give to others. The more you do in your games or social contacts of any form, to give others a good time, to make others feel good, the more friends you will have, the more you will be invited out, the more opportunities for enjoyment will come to you. You can make every tennis session you have, for instance, whether you enjoy it or not, more enjoyable for your partner by controlling your outbursts, by not criticizing yourself, and by being complimentary about your partner's good shots. The same applies to any situation, no matter what it is.

Few people will question the good sense of this letter; but what a tragedy it represents! It is an attempt to do by logic and reason what should have been done by religious education and unreasoning discipline at least eight years earlier. The strategic time to teach children to subordinate their impulses to higher values is when they are too young to understand, but not too young to accept. When parents decide not to send their children to Sunday School until they are old enough to know what it is all about, they are adopting a principle which, if generally applied, is ruinous. For by the time children have learned what it is all about it is often too late for them to do much about it. Many valuable years have been lost.

VII

LOVE AND MARRIAGE

Let the husband render unto the wife due benevolence: and likewise also the wife unto the husband. 1 CORINTHIANS 7:3.

VII

DOROTHY DIX, for many years, has been giving sounder advice on matters of love and marriage than most of the supposedly scientific experts on this subject whose writings have flooded the country. Whereas the latter have emphasized the sexual and emotional aspects of marriage, Miss Dix has consistently emphasized the mechanics of coöperative living. Whereas they have talked about the "frigid" wife, she has described the careless housekeeper. While they discussed the over-sexed man, she has been concerned with the lazy husband. Whereas they have been revealing the meaning of dreams, of suppressed desires, of the thwarted libido, she has been telling wives to be good cooks, husbands to give their wives an honest allowance, and both to act like adults with a job instead of like children with a toy balloon.

In the first few years of my work with individuals, I was myself considerably influenced by the emphasis on the physical aspects of marriage. However, I have since learned that sexual maladjustment is one of the less frequent causes of unhappy marriages. Moreover, the frequency with which this cause is a factor can be attributed, in many instances, directly to the false emphasis on

115

sex encouraged by the pseudo-scientific doctrines of the Freudian school. Obviously, this emphasis would not only bring into the open genuine cases of maladjustment but actually create such maladjustments in the minds of individuals seeking a cause to justify their unhappiness.

My studies indicate that the intimacies of sex are more easily and more often mastered than the hundred and one less private forms of behavior which can make or break a marriage. In other words, character and an unselfish personality and the many good habits they involve are far more important than the details of sex, and require infinitely more practice before they can be mastered. Studies by investigators who do not begin with the assumption that sex is all-important, increasingly confirm this conclusion. One of the most authoritative students in this field, Dr. Bernard Sachs, past president of the New York Academy of Medicine and one of the country's foremost neurologists, has said recently: [1] "Altogether too much attention has been paid and is being paid to the question of sex, to the neglect of other far more important factors. . . ." And also: "Much is said about this oversexed age of ours, oversexed chiefly in the amount of talk about it. Many of the groups, instead of spending hours on sex education could spend time more profitably if they would consider how to develop in children absolute honesty, truthfulness, respect for authority, patriotism, love for one's neighbor."

The emphasis on sex, and its corollaries—the trial marriage, the finding of an affinity, the right to physical

[1] New York, January 15, 1936.

satisfaction in marriage, have distracted attention from the more important meaning of marriage. In the larger sense, marriage is a step by which two imperfect individuals unite their forces in the struggle for happiness. They establish their own small social unit in order that they may better cope with society at large. Marriage is a step in the normal development of the individual, psychologically as well as biologically. It is an opportunity for happiness, not a gift. We cannot demand success in marriage any more than in any phase of life; we must achieve it. The finality of marriage and its vows, as expressed by the rituals of the churches, rightly emphasizes the fact that marriage is an obligation to create a better life, not an experiment in compatibility.

The great difference in these viewpoints is illustrated by the following incidents. A professional colleague, in a field closely allied to psychology, described to me several of his cases in which his recommendation had been against marriage. One of them, typical of the rest, was that of a young woman who had been courted persistently for eight years by a man who was acceptable in every respect. She thought sufficiently well of him to permit his continued suit, and had several times set a date for their marriage. On each occasion, however, she had managed to escape the event, either through an illness of her own, or an illness in her family, or through some emergency which required her presence.

Finally, the man concluded that she was hindered by fears which needed to be forcibly overcome. Deliberately, he devised a situation which he felt would bring

117

her to compromise. The event did precipitate matters, but in the sense that she sought the advice of my colleague as to whether she should now marry this man or not. After a series of discussions, he found that she had been deeply devoted to her father and now compared all other men with him. A father attachment, he concluded, was the root of her aversion to marriage. "I advised her against marrying this man," he told me, "or any man, because no matter whom she married, she would always suffer from the subconscious belief that she was married to her father."

In contrast to the type of case just described, I remember a man who came one day, almost breathlessly, to ask me whether he should go through with his marriage which was scheduled for the following week. "The wedding invitations are out," he told me, "and all the preparations have been made, and I hate to disappoint the girl and her family. But I am afraid I can't make the marriage a success. I don't know whether to go through with it or not. What would you advise?"

One word of encouragement from me would have given him the strength to avoid the marriage. I asked him whether he had had a medical examination assuring him of his physical fitness for marriage, and found that he had. I inquired about the young woman he was to marry, her family, and many circumstances bearing on the marriage. All of them appeared highly favorable. In view of the fact that the bridegroom was anything but prepossessing or able, it seemed like a very fortunate marriage for him. He was timid, introverted, a spoiled child, fearful of life generally. He was certainly not the ideal husband. This marriage, with its resulting stimuli and pressing obligations, might be the making of him. So, as strongly as I could, I urged him to accept this situation as a fortunate opportunity to make a new start in life.

Who was I, to interject my theories of whether this man would be happy or not, between two people who had agreed to face life together? What right had I to discourage this man, already inclined to fear life, from undertaking one of the great extroverting experiences of life? Even though his personality was decidedly below average and his chances for achieving happiness slim, in my opinion, by what authority could I deny him at least the opportunity for happiness, or in effect, tell his bride to wait for a more perfect mate?

In situations like this, where a person's previous life has created obstacles to marriage, fears of happiness, uncertainty of the future, but where the individual has been pronounced medically or physically fit, I have usually advised the struggle for improvement rather than the guarantee of perfection, the adventure of achievement rather than the certainty of success. Marriage is one of the most important steps in the development of an unselfish or extrovert personality. It is better, in my opinion, to have made the attempt and failed, than not to have made the attempt at all.

Indeed, I have a great deal of respect now for the old-fashioned procedure by which parents selected mates for their children, and then told the young couples to make the best of it. The privilege of selecting one's own mate

119

or marrying at one's pleasure is by no means an un-mixed good, especially for the many who postpone marriage to their detriment, and the many who should be or wish to be married but are unable.

In this connection there has been an interesting change during recent years in the attitude of young college women toward marriage as a career. Some years ago, when the feminist movement was at its height, a considerable proportion of college women would generally vote for a business or professional career as their first choice. Within the past three years I have, in connection with certain nation-wide studies among college students, asked the young women such questions as: What career in life is most important to you? Do you consider marriage and helping a husband in his career more important, less important, or equally as important as an independent career of your own? From ninety to ninety-five per cent of the college women have answered that a career as a wife and mother was their primary aim, and that helping a husband in his career was more important than a career of their own. The growing belief among college women that the making of a home, the raising of a family, and furthering the career of a husband, were in themselves a career of major importance indicates a wholesome return to fundamentals. It is unfortunate, however, that so many less than ninety per cent of the college women succeed in marrying—indeed, a lower per cent than of the population at large are married.

The achievement of a happy marriage, even to the selection of a good wife or husband, begins in child-

120

hood. All the elements that enter into the development of a good personality—its emotional poise, its breadth of social pursuits, its adventurous courage in meeting life, its extrovert habits generally, contribute to the finding of a mate and to the success of a marriage.

In simple terms, the girl who learns to play tennis is more likely to find a husband than the girl who does not. The boy who takes part in school dramatics is more likely to find a wife than the boy who prefers listening to the radio or reading about romance. Children who practice musical instruments and get into school orchestras or are able to amuse their friends will have wider opportunities for selecting mates than do those who only listen. Children who learn to dance, play bridge, ping pong, etc., whether they like or not, will meet more eligible mates than serious students who consider such pursuits trivial. Those who are active in Scout groups, go to Sunday School, belong to the young people's society, and who obligate themselves to groups of people even though they do not like all the individuals, are more likely to marry than are the stay-at-homes. I have told hundreds of clients that the way to meet desirable friends is to associate with people to whom they are indifferent.

Neither tennis, dramatics, nor any one of the activities mentioned above, is essential to finding a suitable mate, obviously. The question is one of developing a sufficient range of skills and habits to constitute an unselfish personality, a personality whose energies are converted smoothly and naturally into the social activities enjoyed by *other* people. The criterion is again one of

121

extroversion, sacrificing one's own pleasures, frequently, in order to give pleasure to others.

I was highly gratified, recently, to find that the grade school attended by my young daughter made systematic attempts to teach the children good sportsmanship. This school emphasizes games and group activities as the vehicles for teaching the details of sportsmanship. Competitive games including boys, as well as sports for girls or boys only, are systematically taught. Instead of marking its children merely in *deportment,* that is how quiet and obedient they are in class, my daughter's report card showed also her moral progress in competitive sports.

Young people who have learned to play the games of their times, both frivolous and serious, and therefore learned to give and take in the heat of competition, are less likely to err in choosing a mate and more likely to achieve and hold happiness when married. To begin with, they will have a wider range of mates to choose from and a more comprehensive set of standards by which to choose. They will have learned that curly hair, a beautiful figure, an athletic body, perfect features, while highly desirable, are not so important as the things which the individual does with this equipment. Since they are extroverted and emotionally well poised, they will not be so likely to mistake a physical infatuation for a serious love. The introvert, whose life is self-centered and range of contacts narrow, is more likely to idealize a physical infatuation than is the more realistic extrovert. One of the most common characteristics of the introvert is to insist that his passions and prejudices are ideals and

122

principles. Even in the case of the extrovert, love may be blind. All passions are blind except in so far as they are enlightened by experience and guided by ideals which contradict them. The perfect passion is one sanctioned by a set of ideals which is more important than the passion itself. It is not a particular passion, idealized.

Religion not only provides objective ideals for life generally, but the Church has given concrete expression to these ideals in relation to marriage, through its marriage ritual. In essence, this ritual says that marriage is not merely a private passion but a public contract before a Court far higher and more comprehensive than the legal courts of the land. It stresses the obligations of marriage, not its pleasures and privileges. Its ceremonies represent an extrovert setting to what should be a highly extrovert experience.

As in the preparation for marriage, so in its happy conclusion, the traits of an unselfish personality are of supreme importance. By this I do not mean that both the wife and the husband should play tennis, or golf, or love music, or have all their interests in common. It is desirable that they have certain interests in common such as their religion, their church, their children, and at least a few games or activities by which both can entertain friends or be entertained by them. The possible combinations and diversifications of interests in a happy marriage are almost infinite in number. Nothing in the discoveries of psychology that I know of would permit psychologists to prescribe just what combination of interests or characteristics will produce happiness.

Dr. Arthur Frank Payne, in a recent article, states that many domestic tragedies have resulted from the marriage of a brunette wife to a young man who preferred blondes, and that of the few discoveries by the science of psychology which have stood up under repeated testing, one is that each individual has a "marriage partner pattern." Fortunately for mankind, psychologists have not yet discovered and, in my opinion, never will discover the exact patterns by which to guarantee a happy marriage. What they have discovered are characteristics in individuals which will help to *make* a marriage happy. An extrovert or unselfish man can make either a blonde or a brunette happier than can a selfish man. An introvert can make a beautiful wife or a homely wife equally miserable. However, a self-centered man may marry an unselfish woman, or vice-versa, and both be happy. Indeed, two introverts may marry and achieve happiness, if, through the responsibilities of marriage, the rearing of children, and the making of a place for their family in the community, they become more unselfish. Marriage, from a psychological standpoint, is the union of two imperfect individuals in the struggle for perfection. The direction of their development is more important than what they are at the moment of marriage.

Recently, certain psychologists have published the results of an intensive study of the factors affecting the success of marriage.[2]

[2] Personality Characteristics of Happily Married, Unhappily Married, and Divorced Persons; W. B. Johnson and Lewis M. Terman, Stanford University; Character and Personality, Vol. 3, No. 4, pp. 290-311.

They gave a personality test, such as I have frequently referred to in earlier chapters, and also a test of *interests*, to 116 divorced couples, and 346 married couples. Outstanding among the findings of this study was the fact that the divorced and the unhappily married couples were more unstable emotionally, more introverted, and less self-sufficient than the happily married. Divorced women, particularly, stood out in comparison with the other groups. They were "little given to social service, uplift interests, and 'causes' generally." They expressed much less liking for picnics, conventions, excursions, for the soliciting of funds, and similar pursuits involving an active interest in people.

Happily married men and women, as compared with the divorced and the unhappily married, both husbands and wives, had greater emotional poise, were more extrovert, more aggressive socially, and more self-sufficient. They were more interested in uplift activities and in doing things with other people generally. In short, the traits and habits which I have discussed elsewhere as essential to a good personality were the traits conspicuously shown by the happily married, and conspicuously less present among those unhappily married or divorced.

Summarizing these results in the homely terms of everyday life, the happily married people were the more unselfish, whereas the unhappily married and divorced were the more selfish. Both in these general terms, and in respect to the specific activities followed by each group, we see the application of basic religious values in the achievement of a happy marriage.

One of the most interesting results of this study was the finding that "The divorced, both men and women, have more intellectual interests than either of the married groups." These intellectual interests include the liking for psychology, philosophy, chess; a greater liking for *The New Republic* and less for *The American Magazine,* a greater liking than the other groups for political radicals, and less for Y.M.C.A. work and Bible study.

In short, this study confirms, in relation to a happy marriage, the discoveries of psychologists of the great harm done generally by the emphasis on the intellectual aspects of life at the expense of the homely virtues of living. In marriage, as elsewhere, people may become the fools of reason.

VIII

SOCIAL PLANNING

For every tree is known by his own fruit. For of thorns men do not gather figs, nor of a bramble bush gather they grapes. A good man out of the good treasure of his heart bringeth forth that which is good; and an evil man out of the evil treasure of his heart bringeth forth that which is evil. LUKE 6:44, 45.

VIII

SOCIAL PLANNING

ONE of my most difficult cases was that of a young woman who was involved, with her mother, in a continuous quarrel with the rest of the family. These quarrels centered around the ownership of their house and other financial matters, and were becoming increasingly bitter. A breaking up of the family seemed imminent. The young woman and her mother were planning to leave the father and three sons and then to institute legal proceedings for the possession of the house. In obtaining the histories of the people involved, it appeared that the young woman in question was an ardent advocate of World Peace, and her principal social activities centered in a society for the prevention of war. She had taken part in many demonstrations against war.

"How do you expect to stop war between nations when you can't stop them in your own family?" I was tempted to ask her. It would have been useless, and I shortly withdrew from this case because the hatreds and bad habits of all the people concerned were so deep-seated as to be beyond my influence.

The psychologist finds the seeds of war, poverty, and discontent deep-seated in the inferiority, selfishness, and emotional instability of the individual. He finds the son at war with the father from whose bounties and mistaken generosity he has failed to achieve independence. He sees the daughter suspicious of her acquaintances because she has failed to cultivate the social habits for making them friends. He finds an individual hypercritical of organized social groups because he is too selfish to make the sacrifices necessary for his enjoyment of such groups. He finds a person at war with himself, intellectually and emotionally, because he has failed to subordinate his personal values to a set of higher values irrational though they may seem.

One of the most common symptoms of an inferiority complex or of personal failure is the desire to change the social order, usually in one's immediate environment, often in the world at large. The youngsters, suffering from personal failure, often want to change their families, not themselves. The student who fails in his studies wants to change his teachers or the marking system, not himself. The employee who fails to get the desired salary wants to improve his employer, not himself. The worker, unable to get or hold a position, wants to change the system generally.

Too often to be a coincidence, in my experience, individuals who have failed to achieve social mastery in their own environment want to become social workers and improve the environment of others. It is a curious and significant fact that the field of professional social work, in which many of the movements for social reform have originated, requires its workers to have a college education and two or three years' post-graduate schooling, but does not require them to possess the personality traits or emotional balance necessary for success in normal life. I have discouraged hundreds of ambitions to do social work because they represented the individual's escape from the necessity of improving himself.

Evidences of these symptoms, arising in my experience with cases, are repeated in society at large. Indeed, it has seemed for the past several years as though the whole country were suffering a radical inferiority complex. We have blamed our misfortunes on the bankers, on Wall Street, on the Republicans or the Democrats, on the delinquency of foreign debtors, on the capitalistic system, on the rich, on technology and over-production— in fact on everything and everybody except ourselves, our own past follies and the selfishness which has governed individuals of low as well as high estate.

Certain plans for social reform have, in recent years, gained tremendous followings because they are based on this psychological weakness in so many people. The plans I refer to are those calculated to protect the individual not only against his own failures, passions, and bad habits, but against the vicissitudes of life generally. Millions of people, unable to plan their personal or family economy, are now enthusiastic for a Planned National Economy. Strange how a few capital letters can transform a knotty personal problem into a plausible panacea for society.

In so far as such social reforms become a permanent part of the social structure, they will destroy the very people they are intended to save. The mechanism of this

131

destruction is the process of depriving the individual of the responsibility for himself and his own deeds. It is the same mechanism which we see operating in families, where parents continue to assume responsibility for their children after they should be independent. What happens to the child will happen to a nation of citizens.

Some of these reforms have been labelled as efforts in behalf of the *forgotten man*. Psychologically, the only forgotten man is the man who forgets himself and who delegates the responsibility for his happiness to others.

In my work with adults and young people I find it desirable often to explain beforehand what a psychologist can and cannot do for them. Many come with the hope that they can delegate their problems to me, and that I will find a painless solution. This hope is natural, but furthermore, has been fostered by the theories of psycho-analysis which encourage the individual to project his complexes on the analyst. For example, if a young woman has an Oedipus complex, let her fall in love with the psycho-analyst, who will then reverse the libido in the right direction.

My explanation often runs as follows: "If you have a cold or some other physical ailment, a doctor can usually give you a prescription—a spoonful every two hours, or alternating kinds of pills every three hours—which you may find an easy and pleasant cure. Or, he may put you on an operating table and painlessly remove your appendix or set a bone, after which you lie in bed and have a pleasant convalescence.

"A psychologist cannot perform such simple cures

132

with a psychological problem. He cannot remove bad habits by cutting them out of your brain nor can he graft desirable habits to your present equipment. He may be able to diagnose your problem and make certain valuable suggestions as to things you should do, but you and only you can carry these suggestions into practice. Often these suggestions involve your doing the very things you now dislike doing or find unpleasant.

"When I have finished my examination and made my diagnosis, and you agree with it, I shall ask you to do one or two things calculated not to be too difficult in your situation. If you can bring yourself to do these things, then you will be started on the road to improvement, and then when you come back, we shall outline a program for further action. If you are unable to do these first things, then you had better not come back to me because I, as a psychologist, can do nothing further for you. I can advise, but only you can cure."

As a result of this practice, I see many individuals only once, but some I have seen at irregular intervals for several years. While I was writing this chapter, a man came to see me whom I had examined a year ago. He had been sent originally by his physician, because a whole series of medical examinations had failed to reveal any physical causes for the spells of extreme exhaustion from which he suffered.

My examination showed him to be a great tangle of fine habits and yet decidedly lacking in many of the simple habits of normal living. His fits of fatigue incapacitated him for a steady job, or at least he thought so. My opinion was that he suffered from an unusual excess of energy inadequately expressed. My verdict in this case was apparently brutal, namely, that unless he could get a job and stick at it for a year, there was nothing that I could do for him.

When he came to see me again it was to report that he had gotten a job assembling radio parts and was still holding it almost a year later, in spite of occasional periods of exhaustion which kept him at home several days at a time. Now he wanted to know what to do further, because recent medical examinations had found him in excellent health.

At my suggestion, he mapped out a program of activities for his non-working hours, including a night a week at the Young Men's Hebrew Association, one visit a week either on his wife's family or his own family, one evening for taking his wife to the movies or a restaurant, and one evening for games of some kind with acquaintances and friends. One evening was to be devoted to complete exhaustion, if he felt like it, but none was to be given over to his principal ambition, which was to study. He had already studied books too much and people too little. He has since reported satisfactory progress in carrying out this program and he may yet acquire enough normal habits of expressing his energies to make periods of exhaustion unnecessary.

Some of my colleagues tell me that I am too radical in my insistence on the independence of the individual, especially those who encourage frequent professional visits by their clients. My answer is that I would rather have my clients make their own mistakes than plan their mistakes for them. Indeed, I have told hundreds that it is better for them to make seven mistakes than to make one. There is little doubt that the trend of psychological practice is to make the individual responsible for himself, his actions and his happiness.

Any normal person may require temporary assistance, psychologically as well as medically, spiritually, or financially. The depression made many independent people temporarily helpless. But to convert such difficulties into a long drawn-out or permanent program of dependence, whether done by a psychologist or by the state, is a crime against the individual and against those who must support him. It is comparable to encouraging the person to sell his most precious birthright for a mess of pottage, and it robs society of the kind of people who make a self-sustaining social order possible.

The religious doctrines of Christ, as can be seen by the most casual student, were concentrated on the individual and not on a new social order. The findings of psychology are serving our rediscovery of Jesus as a far more profound thinker than the popular leaders of today. Christ was not a social reformer, he was a reformer of men. For him, the important social order was the Kingdom of God, to which people were admitted on their individual merits, and not because the Kingdom owed them a living. Steadfastly and painstakingly, he refused to identify himself with any social schemes. When asked whether it was lawful to pay tribute to Caesar, his answer was: "Render therefore unto Caesar the things which are

Caesar's; and unto God the things that are God's." He condemned the Pharisees, but on religious grounds, and because of their empty rituals. He criticized the rich not because they had wealth but because they put wealth above everything else.

He saw in riches a great obstacle to character, but his parables of the king and his unmerciful servant (Matthew 18:23-34); the laborers in the vineyard (Matthew 20:1-17); the talents (Matthew 25:14-30); the good steward (Luke 12:42-48); the dishonest land agent (Luke 16:1-13); the master and servant (Luke 17:7-10); the nobleman and the pounds (Luke 19:12-27) reveal a genuine sympathy with the ownership and production of wealth, and a keen appreciation of the mutual obligations of servants and masters, laborers and lords. To the disciples he said: "Seek ye first the Kingdom of God and all these things shall be added unto you." He drove the money-changers out of the temple, but he did not appropriate their money. He supped with the rich and he fed the poor, but while he encouraged the rich to give to the poor, he nowhere encouraged the poor to envy the rich—in fact, quite the contrary. When he was brought to trial before Pontius Pilate, no evidence could be produced to prove that he had advocated a new social order, or any kind of security which did not grow out of the character of the individual himself.

While not indifferent to the material comforts of life, Christ's great contribution was to make individuals independent of and superior to any material standard of living and loyal to the laws of their personal integrity.

136

In this respect he was the prototype of the Pilgrims who settled New England, the pioneers of the covered wagon, of the wealthy Washington at Valley Forge, of Lincoln educating himself before a log fire, of Goodyear starving himself to perfect rubber, and of the galaxy of men and women who make the history of America something we look back on with a glow.

Many prominent clergymen and representatives of the Church have vigorously defined the current issues between a materialistic and a religious conception of life. "No form of economic reorganization," says one, "will work any better than this one works, without a deeper thing." "The desire for money and leisure," says another, "are the two false idols of the twentieth century." "Christ emphasized the values, not the certainties of life," says another. "We have set up a God in our own image, a god of greed, covetousness, and irresponsibility. We have the Commandments and the Gospels, but the Church needs a new Moses to preach them and to bring the people to their senses and their popular idols to the dust."

And yet, other religious leaders and whole groups of clergymen have expressed totally different conceptions. One prominent clergyman is said to have enlisted ten million followers through his talks on the redistribution of wealth and a central banking system. At a service I attended, the pastor read a resolution voted by the General Council of the Congregational and Christian Churches of the United States, as follows:

137

Social Gospel and Economic Problems

VOTED by vote of 130 to 17: 1. Whereas, we commit ourselves with hearty avowal of the faith of our fathers to walk in all God's ways known or to be made known to us, and with sincere passion, which we believe derives from our Master, to make abundant life available to all men everywhere.

Whereas, our present competitive profit-seeking economy shows itself to be increasingly self-destructive and,

Whereas, it depends for its existence upon exploitation of one group by another, creates industrial and civil strife and international war, precipitates periods of unemployment, perpetuates insecurity and all its attendant miseries, and progressively curtails the cultural and educational opportunities of our people, thus destroying human values, moral and spiritual, and

Whereas, these flagrant social evils exist side by side with potential natural abundance, which the present economy is unable to utilize and distribute, however much good it may have done in the past and however honest and idealistic, individuals dependent upon the system may be,

Be it Resolved that:

We set ourselves to work toward:

The abolition of the system responsible for these destructive elements in our common life, by eliminating the system's incentives and habits, the legal forms which sustain it, and the moral ideals which justify it.

The inauguration of a genuinely coöperative social economy democratically planned to adjust production to consumption requirements, to modify or eliminate private ownership of the means of production or distribution wherever such ownership interferes with the social good.

And be it further Resolved that:

We encourage the study of our local churches of these and

138

related economic problems for their social and moral implications.

This program of social reform, similar to many others
formally expressed by religious bodies, seems to me
diametrically opposed to the teachings of Jesus. If Jesus
were present today, judging by his works while living, he
would house the destitute in the empty churches, he
would inspire the employed to help the unemployed and
the fortunate to share the sufferings of the less fortunate.
He would approve the block or neighborhood relief plan.
He would persuade the rich and the competent to give
their money and experience to plans for wise employment. He would convert suffering into spiritual strength
and personal self-reliance. He would help in material
things, as he often did, but he would promise no security
in a material world. To rich and poor alike he would
preach the eternal values of a higher Kingdom as the
key to a more abundant life in our temporal world. *Instead of institutionalizing the weak he would humanize
the strong.*

Such speculations are based on my conception of
religion and Christianity, which many others share. But
speaking as a psychologist, often confronted by individuals trying to rationalize their weakness, the resolution
quoted above is a perfect example of defeat and inferiority. It says, plainly: We, the ministry, have failed
in the mission of Jesus. We have failed to inspire our
people with the belief in God, the belief in the Ten Commandments, and the observance of the Gospel of Christ.
Since we have been unable to instil in people the basic

139

habits of religion, the economic system must be at fault. Therefore, we advocate changing the economic system.

How this is to be done without violating the basic principles of religion is a problem left unanswered.

In any case, this is not the road to the abundant life as the psychologist sees it, nor the religion that inspires my return. I should be of little help to young people in their educational problems if I told them that the educational system must first be revised; or to people who cannot make friends, by telling them that the social values were all wrong; or to those who cannot hold a job that the business structure needed revamping. No doubt our social-economic institutions are imperfect, but they can be brought nearer perfection only by individuals who are themselves more perfect.

If the people seek God and a restatement of the Ten Commandments and the teachings of Jesus, will the ministry give them a "social economy planned to adjust production to consumption requirements," or a scheme for the "socialization of credit"? "If ye then be not able to do that thing which is least, why take ye thought for the rest?" Luke 12:26.

IX

THE VICE OF EDUCATION

Let no man deceive himself. If any man among you seemeth to be wise in this world, let him become a fool, that he may be wise. For the wisdom of this world is foolishness with God. 1 CORINTHIANS 3:18.

IX

THE VICE OF EDUCATION

ALTHOUGH my professional experience has been confined to normal people, or people whose departure from the normal had not reached pathological or medical dimensions, it includes a considerable number of individuals troubled by bad sexual habits or other recognized vices. However, by far the most common vice among my clients is one not generally thought of as such, namely, the vice of too much education and culture.

The worship of formal education is one of the outstanding phenomena of American history. In 1889, the total number of students enrolled in colleges throughout the country was 55,687. In 1934 it was 975,218 or about twenty times as many.[1] In 1918 one third of all children in the United States received all or part of a high school education. By 1933 the proportion had risen to one half. In recent years the trend has been towards an even more rapid increase in the number of high school and college students. Aside from the natural trend, certain movements for social and economic reform are hastening this growth. A college education or its equivalent for every child is a widely heralded goal.

[1] U. S. Commission of Education Records, 1901–2, p. 1612; School and Society, Vol. 40, pp. 785 and 861.

The purpose of this widespread education is to develop the individual and to prepare him for life. And yet, certain experiments made by psychologists during the past five years prove that formal education above the grade school does little or nothing to improve personality or character. More specifically it has been found:

That the people with practically no education have personality or personality traits equal to those of college graduates.

That the poorer students in a high school or college stand as high in personality traits as do the much better students.

That people who have the highest scholastic intelligence as measured by tests of scholastic capacity are just as likely as not to be lowest in personality traits as measured by such tests as Thurstone's Personality Schedule, Root's Extroversion and Introversion, Allport's A-S Reaction Study, Bernreuter's Personality Inventory, and my own test of personality traits of adolescents. Those who are lowest in intelligence tests are just as likely as not to rank highest in personality traits.

That although the personality of some students improves during the high school or college ages, that of others deteriorates, so that the net result is zero. In other words, there is no average improvement of personality due to education.

One of the most extensive studies in this field is that based upon the 10,000 individuals examined by the Adjustment Service referred to in the first chapter. When these individuals were grouped in accordance with their education and their performance in tests of certain personality traits, it was found that college students were not significantly superior to high school students, or high school students to grade school pupils in respect to the personality traits measured.

There is no body of evidence in the whole field of psychology that proves any definite growth of character or personality as a result of higher education in its generally accepted forms. There is a growing body of evidence that no significant growth in personality is brought about by such education. Indeed, there is some good evidence that the contrary often occurs, and that the prolongation of formal education results in a deterioration of personality.

Although these findings may seem extremely radical, they only confirm what many employers, parents, and even some educators have learned from personal experience. Employers no longer fall over each other in their haste to employ college graduates. Moreover, in making their selections, they are often more influenced by a student's extra-curricular activities and his achievements in dealing with his fellow students, than by his success with his professors.

Speaker Cannon was reputed to have once said to an undergraduate interviewer who asked him what he thought of a college education: "Well, I don't think a college education can do much harm to a young man of average intelligence." Such views, even though held by a considerable number of thinking people, have a limited significance. When their truth is demonstrated by

145

scientific tests, or tests approaching scientific certainty, they challenge the most serious consideration. When widely enough recognized, the long overdue revolution in our comparatively modern traditions of education will quickly take place. Although conventional educators may not realize it, the C.C.C. Camps probably represent the first important stage in the revolution of education in America.

My experience with the educational vices of individuals is obviously not peculiar to me, but symptomatic of a far-reaching state of affairs. The mechanisms by which education retards or deteriorates the personality are illustrated by the following two cases, one extreme and the other more ordinary.

The extreme case was that of a man twenty-nine years old, a chemical engineer who had become discouraged with his profession and who hoped that I would help him decide on a new vocation. This man had graduated from one of the finest engineering schools in the country, had continued on a fellowship awarded for brilliant scholarship, for another two years leading to a master's degree. He had then spent three years at one of the greatest universities of Germany, where he received a doctor's degree for his studies in an abstruse phase of chemistry. Upon his return to this country he had obtained a position in the research laboratories of a leading steel manufacturer.

At the end of a year he was asked to resign his position and the reason given was that he lacked sufficient skill in preparing and setting up the technical apparatus

146

required in his experiments. My client admitted the truth of this statement and felt that it was an obstacle which would prove insurmountable in any of his further attempts in his field, including teaching. He hoped that I could discover some other aptitude in him which might lead to another vocation, and one of the fields he had thought of was psychology.

Here was a pathetic case of defeat and actual despair, due to the prolonged postponement of contact with realities. Tests showed that this man had at least average capacities for mechanical work, and if he had found it necessary to develop this ability earlier, he might have done so in spite of his disinclination for manual work. Instead, he had followed the easier course, acquiring more and more theory, which he liked, and avoiding more and more its application, which he disliked. When his education should have begun bearing fruit, he was helpless. Now, although a fine-looking man, with a pleasant personality on the surface, he lacked confidence, he lacked force, he was indecisive, he had developed many introvert habits. His personality and his capabilities had been seriously impaired by his years of study and by the false satisfaction of academic achievement.

A more fortunate individual, but one headed for a similar fate, was a recent college graduate just on the point of choosing his career. He had come east to look into the possibilities of a school in journalism at one university, a dramatic school at another university, and a department of English at still another. His family was

147

sufficiently affluent to permit his going on with two or three years more of study.

His father, it appeared, was a hard-headed business man who wanted his son to go to work immediately. The mother, however, was of the intellectual type, and wanted her son to follow one of the scholarly professions. She, and his college education, had influenced him strongly in this direction and imbued him with a dislike for the materialism of the everyday world. "I am anxious," he said, "to achieve and enjoy the higher cultural values of life. I don't want to grub for money, and I don't care to be a great success financially. My favorite subject is English. I have done some writing but not for publication. I like dramatics. I think I might teach, or study journalism, or go in for playwriting. I can't tolerate the thought of sacrificing these cultural interests to the exhausting grind of a stifling business career."

Psychological tests showed that his scholastic capacities were only average, though he did have some flair for English and showed some promise in journalism. Most conspicuous, however, was his hesitant and flabby personality. Although a very attractive-looking boy, with pleasing manners, there was no spark, no enthusiasm, no force. His ideas were nebulous and even his speech was halting.

I did not try to discourage his desires for culture, and even encouraged his belief in the possibilities of journalism as a career. However, I urged him as much as I could, legitimately, to get a job first—possibly with a magazine, a newspaper, with an advertising agency; but

148

at least a job, any kind of a job. I pointed out, what was obvious even to him, that his personality had become spongy, and if he went on with his education, he would still remain a sponge. What he needed was to develop powers of contraction, or the habits of translating his energies into useful forms of expression under the pressure of competitive life. When he had developed some of these habits, then he could profitably study journalism and, incidentally, have something to write about.

After about six months he returned to tell me about the job he had obtained with a magazine and had been doing ever since. "I have never been happier in my life!" he exclaimed. "Of course, it is not much of a job, but I am learning a great deal about people and work that I never knew before. Much of the time I am clipping and pasting articles, but whenever it gets monotonous I remember your last remarks: 'A job, any kind of a job, even if it is only that of a hod-carrier, or errand boy, or wrapping parcels, will do things for you that you need to have done.' My job is better than these, and it certainly has given me a clearer and more happy outlook. I am going to take a night course in journalism this winter."

The change in this boy's appearance and behavior was amazing. He was enthusiastic, he talked fluently and with conviction, he radiated confidence and purpose. His energies had begun to turn outward.

I have helped many young people, on the basis of aptitudes revealed by psychological tests, to map out an educational plan. On the other hand I have discouraged hundreds from carrying out the plans they had in mind, and nearly always because their personalities could not afford a continuation of the process of absorption. They needed to become acquainted with people in the flesh rather than with people in books. They needed to test the theories they had rather than to learn about new theories. Instead of applying themselves to the pursuit of knowledge they needed to apply the knowledge they had to the pursuit of a livelihood. They needed to stop sponging, which they enjoyed doing and which was becoming a vice, and needed to start producing, which they increasingly dreaded.

There are many good reasons to explain the findings of psychologists in respect to the harmful effects of education. In my files are over one hundred clippings of statements by noted educators and groups appointed to study education which point out the faults in our present educational system. However, I shall confine my statements to the causes revealed by my experiences with individuals and to the results of studies made by other psychologists.

The process of developing an effective personality is the process of acquiring extrovert habits, already described. It consists of acquiring skills which increasingly convert the energies of the individual into useful and satisfying channels. The child is predominantly a consumer; it consumes or absorbs more than it produces. The effective personality must be primarily a producer, producing more than it consumes. In other words, the effective person must acquire a predominance of skills which will be pleasing and useful to other people first,

150

and only secondarily satisfactory to himself. The world gives itself to the child. The personality must give itself to the world.

Education, while it helps cultivate many desirable and extroverting habits, is essentially a period of absorption. The habits it cultivates most are the habits of listening, reading, and studying. The longer this process continues, the more these habits of absorption become fixed and elaborated. As the habits of absorption are elaborated by high school, college, post-graduate and extension courses, the habits of production are often curtailed or deferred. Increasingly the individual is prepared to learn more, to read more, to listen more, and to do less. The habits of absorbing, the introvert habits, become so predominant that, upon graduation, the student often has no idea of what he should do next. One of my clients, an undergraduate in one of our great eastern colleges, re-marked that it was considered bad form to ask a senior what he was planning to do after graduation. Even when students have a vocation in mind, it often takes them years to acquire the basic work habits required in their fields.

In many cases in my experience, the habits of absorp-tion had reached the proportions of a vice, a vice for continued education, for culture, for an intellectual life, which proved the greatest obstacle to developing effective and creative personalities. One of the common symptoms of the over-educated, ineffective personality is an interest in psychology or the reading of books which he believes represent psychology. Since the wheels of his energy

151

turn only on themselves, he becomes interested in learning what makes them go round, a typical introvert tendency. The extrovert, or the person with enough desirable skills, does not have to study psychology. He practices it. Habits that are sound from a psychological point of view can no more be acquired from books on psychology than can the habits of golf from a book on golf, or the skills of swimming from a book on swimming. I have warned probably more than a thousand people against the excessive reading of psychology. There is no more reason for the extensive study of psychology by adults than there is for their reading of books on anatomy and medicine. Both habits tend to produce hypochondriacs, and are symptoms of over-education, exaggerated habits of absorption.

Education is comparable to a nursing period. Although its object is to prepare people for useful living, it tends increasingly to prolong the period in which children are kept out of the stream of actual living. Except in certain cases of specific preparation, like that for medicine with its inevitable and rigorous interneship, the longer a person is shielded from the realities of a working life, the less able he may be to meet them when the time comes. The hours, the discipline, and the pressure of the work done in schools, represent often a vacation from life rather than a preparation for life. And, sad to say, the relaxation and lowering of school standards, which inevitably results from having to put so many more children through the schools, makes education a picnic for

152

the capable children who might have been benefitted most.

The lowering of school standards in order that a much larger number of pupils may be passed through a given number of high school or college years is a notorious fact. Not only in respect to subjects required but in respect to the performance in those subjects, the poorest students set the pace. The relaxation has been especially great in the field of mathematics and the mathematical sciences. This is one group of subjects which psychologists have found to have a favorable effect on personality. Mathematics involves the development of the most precise, most sustained, most closely knit set of habits. In comparison with such subjects as English, the social sciences, the foreign languages, history, etc., the standards in mathematics are far more exact and exacting. The more slipshod the habits which a subject permits, the more harmful it becomes to the development of desirable personality traits. These statements apply to general trends, not to the exceptional pupils who rise superior to the laxities of their educational environment, no matter what subjects or courses they take.

While this section was in preparation, several articles and reports have appeared in print illustrating the tendency to lower educational standards. In New York City the high school requirements in mathematics, foreign languages, and history have been made optional. A responsible committee of twelve important educators after a year of study, have submitted their report in which they recommend that passing grades or marks be abandoned, and that all children be passed automatically from one grade to another regardless of their standing. The effects of such a plan on the work habits and the sense of responsibility among children would be devastating.

The revolt against marks and grades in figures has continued for years, and has become increasingly successful. And yet the marking system is one of the few definite points at which education resembles the actual world with its systems of incentives and rewards, its mixture of justice and human fallibility. I have explained to my own children many times the similarity between this aspect of their education and their future experience. Good marks are obtained in two ways, first by doing good work and second by learning how to please the teacher—the latter is as important as the former. Vocational progress and good wages are achieved not simply by doing good work but by doing it in ways which will please the bosses. One represents a kind of academic intelligence, the other represents intelligence in making personal contacts, that is good extrovert habits of paying attention to the interests and wishes of other people. The latter may be even more important than the former.

Every step in the lowering or relaxation of educational discipline and standards accentuates the role of formal education as a wet nurse and encourages the intellectual and moral sucking habits of its pupils.

With all the years and varieties of education it is a tragedy that so many people should finish without any

154

special fitness and no idea of a vocation. So many come to me for an examination which will help them select a career or discover some hidden talent. They seldom realize that talents are made rather than found, and that the time to consider aptitudes is while there is still time to develop them.

There are two critical points at which capacities and possible talents should be examined, one just before a high school course is decided on, whether it should be a scientific course, a liberal arts course, an industrial trades course, a course in music, art, or a commercial course. The second critical point for a vocational examination is just before deciding upon a college course.

Psychologists have made remarkable progress in testing and diagnosing aptitudes which suggest the kind of education best calculated to develop them. However, such examinations usually require eight to ten hours; whereas the present educational system is better equipped to give its students eight years of the wrong kind of education than eight hours of competent diagnosis.

An effective personality requires not only a variety of skills, but relative superiority in a few fields and distinct superiority in one. The chief superiority should be in a vocational field, the others in the field of sports, hobbies, and the social arts. The frequent cases of inferiority which we find among people today are due almost entirely to the failure to cultivate specific habits of success.

The educational system, by its very nature, tends to discourage the development of specific forms of superiority. It tends to flatten out people's aptitudes rather than

155

to cultivate them. In trying to regiment students for life in general, it fails to develop habits of mastery in specific phases of life. I am not concerned here with the long-standing controversy in regard to the merits of a liberal education and a specialized education. Even a liberal arts college could insist on having its students do intensive and superior work in one set of courses. Conversely, many students coast through an engineering school without being required to do superior work in any one phase of engineering. The issue is one of standards and discipline, not merely one of content or the subject matter of the courses studied.

Even in the high schools and grade schools, superiority or greater effort in a few directions could be made a condition. One child might develop a superior handwriting, another a superiority in geography, another an unusual competence in writing letters, or handling correspondence. So far as possible, the subjects of special stress should correspond with existing aptitudes, but the critical point would be the pressure brought to bear on the child to do extra work, unusually intensive work, and highly disciplined work in a particular field. This is not what is commonly understood as progressive education. The mere habit of developing superiority is a preparation for success in later life.

What actually happens is described in the recent report of a ten-year study of twenty-five hundred boys and girls in the New York public schools, made by the well known psychologist, E. L. Thorndike. These children were given a group of psychological tests at the age of fourteen and their school and employment record then carefully followed for the next ten years. It was found that the present system gave only four months less education to the dullest children than it did to the brightest, and that there was no relationship between the capacities of the children and the kind or amount of education they received. Such treatment is well calculated to develop habits of inferiority instead of superiority, with all the consequent damage to personality.

Many institutions, especially business enterprises for profit, depend for their success upon how well their services satisfy consumers in a competitive market. Their products and services are continually being tested and compared, not only by the buyers but by the business executives who appreciate the need for improvement. The field of education, however, represents a vested interest the nature of which is self-perpetuating. Its products or pupils are not subject to the same rigorous tests, and its standards are largely of its own making. In keeping with its emphasis on intellectual development, its criterion in the selection of teachers is primarily that of academic attainment, namely, the completion of a normal school course or the obtaining of an M.A. or Ph.D. degree.

This process results in what may be described as the inbreeding of the teaching staff. The educational system tends to perpetuate itself and its predominantly intellectual ideals by selecting as teachers those who most closely approximate these ideals. The process is much like that of an accountant who audits his own books and

157

systematizes his own mistakes. Teachers are trained to teach their subjects, not to develop the personalities of their pupils.

A dramatic revelation of this fact is embodied in a psychological study of the personality traits of pupils in eighteen widely separated grade schools. In this study forty teachers were asked to rate the personality traits of their students. When the results were computed, it was found that consistently, the teachers of the fourth grade had rated their pupils higher in personality than the teachers of the fifth grade had rated their pupils. Fifth grade pupils were rated as having better personalities than pupils of the sixth grade. Pupils of each succeeding grade were rated lower in personality. According to the teacher's conception of personality, therefore, the fourth grade pupils had personalities averaging twice as high as the personalities of the ninth grade pupils.

This is a strange phenomenon, in view of the known fact that personality and extrovert habits develop more rapidly between the ages of ten and fourteen than in any other period except the period of one to ten. The truth is that the ideal child, from a teacher's point of view, is the one that fits most quietly and unobtrusively into the narrow range of the classroom routine. The older the child gets and the more it develops an individuality of its own with positive impacts on its environment, the more it invites the critical estimates of its teachers. Inevitably in the present scheme, the teachers' ideal of a good personality is a quietly absorbing sponge, not a positive, creative individual.

158

This study is not the only one of its kind, but one of the latest. It confirms the results of previous similar studies and represents a finding well recognized by students of this phenomenon. This phenomenon is the inevitable result of an educational system in which the intellectual aspects of development are stressed at the expense of all others, and where the selection of teachers is based so largely on formal academic considerations.

A wholesome contrast to the characteristic inbreeding of education is that represented by the medical profession and the education of a physician. In the medical field, teaching is a matter of pride among practicing physicians. Not only are many of the courses in the medical schools taught by practicing doctors, but the whole system of interneship and hospital routine is founded upon the relationship between the student or interne and the practicing physicians who teach him. This field might well serve as an ideal from which to work down into the more common fields of education.

Probably the most damaging single aspect of educa-tion is just the one on which it prides itself most, namely, the creation of a liberal mind. The liberal mind and its corollary, liberalism, are the idols of education. Not only in scientific fields, but in moral, social, religious, and political fields, liberalism is held up as praiseworthy while conservatism is condemned as reactionary.

The process of education is a process of intellectual liberation. Geology proves that the world could not have been created in seven days nor man in one. History describes the mythologies of different religions. Anthropology explains the Ten Commandments as the mores or customs peculiar to a certain race and therefore not binding on another race under different conditions. Philosophy describes the emancipation of the mind from anthropomorphic and religious conceptions of the world. Ethics describes hedonism, stoicism, and the different schools of conduct, leaving the student free to choose his own. These are but a few of the innumerable points at which education emancipates the individual from the prejudices and the traditions of the past.

The doctrine of the liberal mind is a dogma of education which is as mystical and irrational as any dogma of the church ever was. What is the value of a liberal mind, *per se?* Wherein lies the advantage of the ruthless iconoclasm which, in effect, education represents? How is the individual, freed from the beliefs and thought habits acquired in early childhood, better equipped to deal with life? To what higher, more inspiring, more compelling set of ideals has the liberal mind been released? The chief answer to these questions in the past is expressed in the educational dogma, *culture for its own sake,* or, *knowledge for its own sake.* Such a dogma is no less naïve than the dogma of the immaculate conception or the second coming of Christ.

Liberalism, as I have seen it in so many cases, is the result of an indiscriminate releasing of a person from the traditions and restraints of the past without substituting an adequate set of restraints or ideals for the future. It manifests itself clinically among younger people, as follows:

160

In the tendency to regard parents as old fashioned and the older generation at large behind the times.

In the tendency of students to be liberal with their parents' money, automobile, and other property without assuming any corresponding obligations or responsibilities.

In the intellectual scorn which students often show for the religious, political, and moral creeds of their parents and of their own early childhood.

In the repugnance which so many students from humble homes develop toward the occupations of their fathers, and toward the more manual types of vocations.

In the frequent tendency to deprecate business as a career and to idealize an intellectual or more cultural type of occupation, regardless of fitness for such pursuits. Seldom do these young people realize that only the surplus of production and wealth makes education and intellectual occupations at all possible.

Among adults, liberalism often manifests itself in a lack of conviction on matters of basic right and wrong, sometimes described as tolerance. The uncertainty of the parents robs them of their authority with their children. In place of authority they exercise a liberal attitude toward children who are themselves bound to be still more liberal. A tolerant attitude in the home is a corollary to a tolerant attitude toward right and wrong in social and political matters generally. The moral indignation of a Christ driving the money-changers out of the temple is almost completely lost. Even when such moral uncertainty may not lead to great personal unhap-

161

piness, it leads to no positive action in a world so in need of a moral housecleaning.

The more positive and energetic liberals, those who come to represent the Liberal Movement, are probably the most conspicuous products of a liberal education. Having acquired an enthusiastic conviction about some comprehensive plan for mankind, with unbounded confidence in their intellectual powers, they often tend to drive their plan toward immediate execution, disregarding all restraints of traditions. In effect, their theme is: What is old must be wrong, what is new must be right. Property rights, contracts of long standing, the Constitution of the United States, existing institutions, to say nothing of the Ten Commandments and religion generally, belong to the horse and buggy age, and may, therefore, be treated as obsolete. This is the picture in its crude outlines, to be sure, but its pertinence to current phenomena of American life is obvious.

Children who are liberal with their parents' property and Liberals who are free with the lives and property of society stem from the same source. They exemplify the emancipation from traditional restraints without regard to their value in comparison with modern ideas. They represent minds dragged loose from their moorings, plunging confidently in dangerous directions. The more powerful such minds the greater their potential havoc.

There is great need in the field of education for the codification of values and basic truths about human nature; for the preservation and honoring of the noble

162

traditions which the race has acquired; for the subordination of intellectual arrogance to the discipline of the unselfish life. Where, better than in religion, can the basis for such a synthesis of the past with the present be found?

X

THE ABUNDANT LIFE

I am come that they might have life, and that they might have it more abundantly. JOHN 10:10.

But seek ye first the kingdom of God, and his righteousness; and all these things shall be added unto you. MATTHEW 6:33.

X

THE ABUNDANT LIFE

LONG after the children of Israel had been led into the land of milk and honey, a new leader announced: "I am come that they might have life, and that they might have it more abundantly." John 10:10. In our own land of milk and honey, the promise of a more abundant life has assumed a new importance. Indeed, it has become the dominating political, social, and religious theme of our times. We hear it preached on all sides, from every source—high government officials, political leaders, prominent clergy, and advocates of social reform.

To a psychologist dealing with individuals who, in one way or another, are seeking a happier, more abundant life, this emphasis is of unusual interest. The practicing psychologist is necessarily a student of happiness and its causes. He must understand not only the circumstances in a person's environment or in the person himself which have obstructed his happiness; he must also know what steps will help that person to achieve a happier life. Therefore he reads with professional interest the descriptions of the more abundant life set before the American public during the past few years.

One of the definitions, which has now become famous,

is that "a moderately full life for a family under American conditions would cost about $2500 a year." Another is that it requires a $5000 home for each family and a college education or its equivalent for every child. Illustrating the definitions set forth by religious groups or conferences is one which stated that unless incomes of from $3000 to $10,000 were made possible for all families, "the present economic system must declare its intellectual and moral bankruptcy." Other definitions include liberal pensions in old age, a maximum of thirty hours' work a week, compensation for unemployment, and in general all the many provisions calculated to insure individuals an American standard of living at all times and under all circumstances.

Whatever the details, these definitions have one point in common. They all define the abundant life in terms of dollars and the things which money will buy. Such an ideal of the abundant life, from my experiences with individuals, is the most disastrous and destroying ideal which could possibly be offered. The abundant life, psychology proves, can never be defined in terms of money. It can only be defined in terms of habits, that is, character. Happiness never resides in what an individual has, but always in what the individual does. It never consists of what an individual receives, be it much or little, but always of what he gives, not in money but of himself. Certainly it does not reside in an easier life, but in a more active life, especially in old age. Most positively, it does not come from a fine and costly education, but from the personality traits which the individual develops, or, as illustrated by the individuals already described, from the extent to which a person is able to convert his innate energies into good work habits and effective contacts with his fellowmen.

I know of only one among the many comparatively new governmental agencies which is helping people to attain the more abundant life, that is the Civilian Conservation Corps Camps. Here alone, the popular conception of an American standard of living and a life of greater ease has been abandoned. Here, the wages are ridiculously low, and even so, the earner is allowed to keep only a pittance for himself; the rest must go to his family. Here, most men must work harder than they ever worked before, and at tasks whether they like them or not. Here, men feel tired at night and know the pleasure of an earned night's sleep. Here, men must get up in the morning, whether they feel like it or not. They must associate and work with all kinds of people, whether they like them or not. They must eat pork and beans, corned beef and cabbage, or what they get, or go without; but such is their life that simple fare soon tastes good to them. Whatever their social, economic, or political beliefs, their tastes or fancies, catered to by indulgent parents at home, they must conform to the disciplines and routines which these camps embody.

To dozens of spoiled men and spoiled sons of well-to-do fathers, I have recommended the C.C.C. Camps as a step in their rehabilitation. Most of these individuals had considerably more wealth than is currently considered essential to an abundant life. They had jobs, they had money, but they lacked certain important habits. Because they were not destitute, or had no destitute families to support, they were not eligible for the C.C.C. In a few extreme cases, I have suggested a period in the Army or the Navy, with some excellent results.

Indeed, one of my early cases was that of an eighteen-year-old boy who had developed a very damaging set of habits, and was the despair of his parents and even of himself. In the first five minutes of our interview, he told me that he had, during the previous six years, been psycho-analyzed twice, and understood his difficulties and their causes quite clearly. "I have rationalized the situation," he remarked, "but that hasn't helped me to overcome it. I am worse than I ever was." "What you need," I prescribed, "is not *under*standing, but *over*-activity, a minimum of thinking, and a maximum of doing in company with others; a situation in short where other people do the thinking and give the orders, and you do the work. The only place which approximates these conditions and which your family can afford is the Army or the Navy."

The next day the boy's mother arrived in a flurry. "Are you not afraid that he will acquire bad habits in the Army?" was her concern. I tried to explain that the habits he already had were such that the chances were more favorable for his acquiring some good, correcting habits than for his acquiring the flagrantly bad habits she had in mind. There the matter ended, so far as I was concerned, until a few months later the boy walked into my office looking like an entirely different person. "My

170

mother objected to my joining the Army," he explained, "but she did let me go to Camp Dix. It did me so much good, and my improvement was so obvious to her, that she has now withdrawn her objections to my entering the Army. I am certainly on the way, and I stopped in to tell you that I enlisted in the Army yesterday." Of course, Camp Dix was probably far better than the Army for this boy, but it existed for only a few weeks in the year.

Unfortunately, there are in this country practically no institutions based on the principle of enforced work and group discipline, other than those I have already mentioned and our reform schools and penal institutions for criminals. Physicians are rapidly coming to appreciate the therapeutic value of manual work, and are putting people into classes for basket-weaving, wood-working, and metal crafts. Summer camps for young people are gradually adding real work to their camp activities. Such steps, while desirable, are but a pale approach to the enforced, coöperative routine of the C.C.C. Camps.

The men who emerge from the rigid discipline of these camps, it is widely agreed, have not only experienced an abundant life, but are better equipped to achieve a more abundant life. Through their enforced contacts they have learned to respect and like people whom they would never voluntarily have chosen as friends. Having learned, often, to think more highly of their fellow workers, they have also acquired greater confidence in themselves—the latter is a by-product of the former. Through the pressure of mass action they

171

have come to appreciate a day's work at jobs which, left to themselves, they would have spurned at three times the pay. Life in the barracks, in tents, and on army fare, has given them an inkling of the fact that the more abundant life lies, not in the American standard of living or in $2500 a year, but in themselves. Under a discipline which did not consult their whims, they have learned that action is more satisfying than introspection, physical exhaustion sweeter than self-indulgence. They emerge from those camps better equipped to *give* their energies and attention to others and therefore more likely to *receive* a satisfying compensation for themselves. In short, they have become more extroverted.

In sharp contrast with this great institution which, in creating personality also creates physical wealth, we see powerful forces working for the destruction of personality and incidentally the destruction of wealth. Any one who has read the daily newspapers during the past few years must have been impressed by the madness of large sections of the American public and many of its popular leaders for a short cut to the more abundant life. Indeed, the redistribution of wealth has been a far more potent political motive than the creation of wealth.

In six months, ten million people were reported to have enrolled under the banner of the Townsend plan for immediate old age pensions of $200 a month. Whole pages of the newspapers have been devoted to pictures and stories of a few people who have won small fortunes in the sweep-stakes, in which probably millions of others have bought numbers. A dominating note in the war

172

veterans organization has been the bonus. Cities and states have seriously considered organized lotteries as a means of raising revenues. "Drive to legalize all gambling begun in Illinois; U. S. Lottery to be considered in Congress; House Committee to begin hearings tomorrow on Painless Taxation," read the headlines of the newspapers on June 27, 1935. The legalization of gambling has already assumed major proportions.

"Out of Colorado's dust clouds," reports the *Reader's Digest*, "has appeared a new economic rainbow with a pot of gold at the end. The gold may be fool's gold, but that possibility appears of small concern to the multiplying millions who are taking up the pursuit. In less than a month's time, the 'send a dime' chain letter lunacy has reached proportions that classify it as one of the major phenomena of a depression era. Here is epitomized the general confusion as to what is money and value. Here is something historically akin to the tulip madness of Holland and the Mississippi Bubble, because it reveals the morality and mentality of an epoch."

Here is something akin to what enraged Moses when, upon his descent from Mt. Sinai, he shattered the tablets of the Ten Commandments because he found the Children of Israel dancing around the Golden Calf. Moses broke the tablets, but in our times, the people and their leaders, political and religious, are breaking the Ten Commandments themselves, all in the name of a more abundant life. Indeed, we might well say that the American people had evolved a *new dispensation* with respect to the Ten Commandments, somewhat as follows:

173

Ten Commandments for a More Abundant Life

I. The more abundant life requires some stealing if it can be done within the law by the individual, or above the law by a government through which the voter can escape personal responsibility for his acts.

II. The commandment, six days shalt thou labor and do all thy work, is hereby modified to five days and, preferably, a maximum of thirty hours a week.

III. In compensation for the lessened productivity of the shorter day it is now permissible to covet one's neighbor's possessions and to take them by passing the necessary laws, constitutional or otherwise.

IV. The commandment, thou shalt have no other gods before me, is to be interpreted as meaning that the State is supreme, and anything which the State does becomes right, regardless of any religious doctrines to the contrary.

V. The commandment, honor thy father and thy mother, is made permissive instead of obligatory, thereby lessening the dangers of an Oedipus complex and the contrary influence of parents who still adhere to the old-fashioned virtues.

VI. to X. The observance of these commandments is left to the discretion of the individual within the limits of the statutory law.

Partisan minds may immediately seize on this as an indictment of recent political policies, thereby losing sight of the fact that it is a description of certain basic trends in American life and morals. The depression only hastened the development of these trends and prompted their dramatic revelation. They have been in the making

174

for many years, and the Gibbons of the American Republic will undoubtedly trace their development. Such a history will begin with the hardships of our religious forefathers and the rigors of the Puritan mode of life, and then portray the disintegration of the national character so formed through the succeeding waves of immigrants who came for economic reasons and the new generations who contributed to the material prosperity which has all but strangled the nation.

We have heard it said, repeatedly, that capitalism or the capitalistic system has broken down. It is not capitalism but the character of the people under that system which has disintegrated. The speculative mania culminating in the year 1929 was not different, in essence, from the frantic attempts which have been made currently toward a sleight of hand achievement of the more abundant life. The desire to get something for nothing or without serious responsibility was the dominating motive then and is a dominating social and individual motive today. The public at large participated in the speculations of 1929, if not through stocks then through excessive installment buying and other unwise purchases; it is speculating just as madly today in theories of social security, social justice, in horse races, lucky numbers, chain letters, old age pensions and other mechanical devices calculated to produce happiness without pain. So long as the emphasis in American life and manners remains on an American Standard of Living, materially, rather than on a Standard of Character in

175

accord with the transcendent principles of religion, this process of decay will continue.

How can a psychologist, dealing with only a few individuals, dare to make such sweeping statements? Simply because national events and policies duplicate so exactly the incidents and values of individuals. The politician who talks about the national welfare is still the same man who must deal with the welfare of his immediate family. The voter who has ideas on national policies reveals in them the same prejudices and weaknesses which govern his everyday life.

A father who was having great difficulty with his seventeen-year-old son, described this situation: "My son, I believe, has a good mind, but during the last few years his work in school has become increasingly poor. This term he failed in three of his subjects. However, what worries me more, even, than his school work, is his attitude toward life generally. He seems to think that the world and especially his parents, owe him a living. It happens that we live in a well-to-do community. Many of the families are more wealthy than we, and while I have been quite liberal with my son, giving him a generous allowance, good clothes, letting him drive the family car, etc., he is far from satisfied. Now he wants his own automobile, and keeps talking about the many boys in town who have their own car.

"When I ask him to take care of the furnace or the lawn, or to do some other jobs, he tells me that the other boys don't have to do this sort of thing. Although I sometimes get him to do a job, I can never depend on his

176

doing it properly. He has no sense of responsibility or obligation, but he considers his family responsible for making possible anything he wants to do. In fact, his one idea in life is to have fun, and his idea of a good time, so far as I can see, is to do what he wants to do, when he wants to do it, regardless of anybody else. I am terribly afraid he is developing a character which will make him unfit for the world; just as it has already made him unfit for his studies."

I have seen hundreds of people at various ages and stages, the history of whose failure began just like this boy's. So many things had been done for them by their parents, that they had failed to develop the habit of doing things for themselves. They had coveted many things but had acquired ability in few things. They had acted on the principle that their family owed them a living, an education, and luxuries which they regarded as necessities. From such an attitude in the family to the belief that the world owes one a living, is a small step. The basic reason for this belief is that the individual has failed to acquire the habits and character necessary to making his own way in the world.

Although parents have a grave responsibility in such matters, they are handicapped by the circumstances of our luxurious age. When the American standard of living was far simpler and less luxurious among the rich than it is today among the poor, when children had to contribute to the support of the family at an early age, when the years of education were much fewer, when electricity, modern plumbing, automobiles, and the conveniences of today's life were absent, the development of many good work habits and character traits in youth were almost automatically taken care of.

One father I know recently decided not to substitute an oil furnace for his old coal furnace because, he said: "It is almost impossible for me to find enough chores around the house to give my sixteen-year-old son the training in good work habits he should get in his youth. He took care of the furnace last winter, and for the first time had the experience of getting out of bed mornings on his own responsibility. It was a hard task, but it taught him a good deal. I don't want to install an oil furnace until he has mastered this piece of routine. Besides, he is able to earn certain sums in this way which I would otherwise not give him."

In times when people are so well-to-do that even workers on government relief can afford to strike for higher pay, the development of good work habits is a major problem. Parents and schools indulge the children, parents indulge themselves, and the politician seeks to indulge the masses. All the material advantages of our civilization conspire to make our lives easier and our characters weaker. Only the most intelligent and unselfish parents can counteract these harmful influences on their children. And only the sternest morals and religious convictions can safeguard the parents themselves from the easy manners of their environment. The laudable desire to do well by our children, plus the means to do it, too often does them irreparable harm. The sins of

178

the fathers' prosperity are visited upon the children, and upon the children's children, even unto the third and fourth generations.

The children of poor parents have a tremendous advantage in the struggle for character, today as in times gone by, if their parents can resist the insidious doctrine that the world owes them a living and security. If I could make only one recommendation in regard to the American educational system it would be that all boys between the ages of eighteen and twenty-one be compelled to spend a full year in the Civilian Conservation Corps Camps as now constituted, rich and poor alike, and especially college students.

The life of the family is the life of the nation. The abundant life for the individual as well as for a nation of individuals can be achieved only through the personal competence and ideals of each individual. It cannot be obtained through the dependence of a son on his father, or a father on his inherited wealth, or one group of the nation on the wealth of another group, or through the dependence of the people generally on a paternalistic government. If the possessions and gifts of a father can not buy happiness for his children, how can the fathers of our government give happiness to a nation, especially with gifts that do not belong to them?

Among the Ten Commandments, the one specially stressed in the teachings of Jesus was the commandment: Thou shalt not covet. The word *covet* or *covetousness*, judging from my general readings, has practically disappeared from our present-day vocabulary. Instead, we use such words and phrases as: the redistribution of wealth, taxing the *haves* to pay the *have nots*, processing taxes, social credit, etc. In such guise, these forms of covetousness make an insidious appeal to sentimental idealists afraid to face the realities of human nature and the stern conditions under which character and wealth are created.

Covetousness is the death of character and of creativeness. The boy who covets the wealth of his friends or begs his family for money wastes the energy and time in which he might be learning to create his own wealth at any age. By curtailing the habits which create, covetousness kills the power to enjoy wealth obtained from others. It is the creation of wealth in any form, a friend, a newspaper route, a sonata, an apple stand, a painting, a machine, a business, which lies at the root of happiness, not mere possession. Even of friendship Emerson has said: "The price of true friendship is the ability to do without it." A still greater teacher has spoken thus:

"And one of the company said unto him, Master, speak to my brother, that he divide the inheritance with me. And he said unto him, Man, who made me a judge or a divider over you? And he said unto them, Take heed, and beware of covetousness: for a man's life consisteth not in the abundance of the things which he possesseth. ... The life is more than meat, and the body is more than raiment. . . . If ye then be not able to do that which is least, why take ye thought for the rest? . . . For all these things do the nations of the world seek after: and your Father knoweth that ye have need of these things. . . . But seek ye the kingdom of God; and all these things shall be added unto you . . ." Luke 12:13-31; Matth. 6:32, 33.